The Breakthrough Team Player

The
Breakthrough
Team
Player

*Becoming the M.V.P.
on Your Workplace
Team*

Andrew J. DuBrin

American Management Association

New York • Atlanta • Boston • Chicago • Kansas City • San Francisco • Washington, D.C.
Brussels • Mexico City • Tokyo • Toronto

Library of Congress Cataloging-in-Publication Data

DuBrin, Andrew J.
    The breakthrough team player / Andrew J. DuBrin.
        p.   cm.
    Includes bibliographical references and index.
    ISBN 0-8144-7882-4
    1. Work groups.   2. Interpersonal communication.   3. Interpersonal
relations.   I. Title.
    HD66.D83   1995
    658.4'036—dc20   95-12697
                                                      CIP

Printing number

10   9   8   7   6   5   4   3   2   1

349996

To the members
of my family team,
**Drew, Douglas, Melanie,
Rosemary,** and **Clare**

Contents

Acknowledgments

My primary thanks on this project go to my editorial team at AMACOM, Mary Glenn and Richard L. Gatjens. Glenn and I developed the concept for this book in a two-person brainstorming session. Gatjens made optimum use of his editorial expertise and information technology to get this manuscript ready for production.

Thanks also to people I have worked with on a variety of teams, both in consulting with them and in performing my own work. My experience on two teams at the RIT College of Business—the management team and the graduate programs team—was especially helpful.

Introduction

A key organizational reality is that to be successful, you have to be a good team player. Teams of one type or another predominate in today's workplace. To move ahead or hold on to their jobs, most people are compelled to spend at least part of their time in collaborative effort. The collaborative effort I refer to involves many different types of work arrangements calling for cooperation between two or more people. Excluding the self-employed working alone, virtually every reader of this book will spend some time in one or more of the following work arrangements:

- A management team in which a group of executives shares responsibility for running an organization or a substantial chunk thereof
- A department of more than two people in which some joint projects are undertaken
- A work team in which a group of employees takes care of daily work, but with more collaboration than a conventional department
- A self-managing work team in which team members are given substantial authority to govern their own activities and perform many managerial tasks
- A task force or committee to which members are assigned part time to solve a pressing problem, or explore new opportunities for the company
- A project team whereby the members work together for a relatively long time on an activity of major consequence to the organization, such as launching a new product or reengineering the firm

- A quality circle whereby a group of volunteers devotes a few hours per week to improving the quality or productivity of a product or service
- A virtual team in which the members interact by computer, drop in and out as needed, and take turns being a leader

You might argue that some of the above groups are truer teams than the others because a higher level of commitment and collaboration is required. A project, for example, requires higher levels of cooperation among members than does a traditional department calling for occasional joint activity. Although some work groups require more collaboration than others, the team player is an asset to all of them. Without a high level of cooperation and collaboration, a work group will not achieve the status of being a true team. Instead, it will simply be a collection of individuals working alone whose combined output is the simple sum of their individual output. A team, in contrast, achieves synergy.

If 1,000 workers at all levels from chairperson to entry-level worker were polled, about 999 would agree so far—being a good team player is essential for success.

In recognition of the importance of teamwork, this book has two important purposes. The more obvious purpose is to elucidate the myriad ways in which you can become an effective team player, thus enhancing your contribution to the team. Unfortunately, being a good team player takes you only to the point of receiving average salary increases and career progress.

Its second purpose can have a much bigger impact on your career. I will explain how you can be a superior team player, yet at the same time be enough of a standout performer to be recognized for your unique talents. We may all want to be good team players, but who gets the big promotion, an individual or a team? When the headhunters are asked to find a key executive, who is hired, an individual or a team? After the executive is hired, that person may bring in his or her own team, but the team is rarely hired at the outset.

Sports teams operate on the same principle. In team sports such as basketball, baseball, football, and hockey, team play is essential. Yet the standout players are often paid ten times as much as the team players who do not distinguish themselves. Fans also admire good team players, but they collect far more trading cards of individual players than of teams.

Learning to become the *breakthrough team player*—one who contributes mightily to the team effort but still pulls ahead of the pack—requires a careful understanding of team play. You have to be willing to cope with nuances and subtleties. A trap for many bright, ambitious, and impatient people is to readily dismiss information about the dynamics of team play as "common sense." If being a standout team player were common sense, we would not have two common types of organizational casualties. The first type is those people labeled as "poor team players," and therefore dismissed from consideration for promotion. The second type of casualty is those people who are good team players but watch others break loose from the group to achieve bigger organizational rewards.

To enhance your chances of becoming a breakthrough team player, the information in this book is organized as follows:

Chapter 1 explores the key issue of finding the right balance between being a good team player and finding room for individual recognition. Many of us want to satisfy the demands of the organization yet not sacrifice ourselves for the good of the group.

Chapter 2 explains the major attributes and actions of effective team players, such as sharing credit with the team and using the word *we* frequently.

Chapter 3 describes how to avoid the trap of conforming so much to group norms and expectations that you think like everybody else and lose your uniqueness.

Chapter 4 describes the various roles carried out by team players such as informal leader, Knowledge Contributor, Flaw-Finder, and People Supporter. Exploring these roles will enable you to select several that fit your style and circumstance.

Chapter 5 helps you acquire the right mental set for developing cross-functional skills. Such skills are valuable, because today's managers and professionals are supposed to wear multiple hats and work well with people from other disciplines.

Chapter 6 confronts the reality that team structures have

not eliminated the importance of political behavior. Instead, the astute individual develops political skills targeted at team situations. These skills include knowing how to compliment and support teammates, and how to make the team leader feel good.

Chapter 7 deals with the nuts and bolts issue of how to perform well and look good at meanings, thereby attaining individual recognition. Standing out at meetings is essential, because so much of teamwork is conducted during meetings.

The focus of the book then shifts to team leadership, because so many team players get their turn at being a team leader. Chapter 8 describes many actions and behaviors of effective team leaders, aimed mostly at the human aspects of leadership, such as encouraging group interaction.

Chapter 9 describes how an effective leader deals with the task, or problem-solving, aspect of team leadership. For example, suggestions are made for reaching agreement on demanding tasks.

Chapter 10, the final one, synthesizes information in the previous chapters to present a model for achieving individual recognition, yet remaining an excellent team player. Although not widely recognized, finding this balance is a major challenge facing career-minded people.

My approach in this book is to present you with sensible, workable ideas to help you become a breakthrough team player. Many of the ideas are based on my own experience in working with teams and being a team leader. Many other ideas are based on the research and observations of others. My approach takes the form of giving advice and making suggestions, rather than asking you to wade through the theory, research, and case analysis behind my ideas.

The Breakthrough Team Player

1

Walking the Tightrope

Being described by others as a good team player is a workplace accolade. The executive who works cooperatively with other members of the top management team is heralded as a fine team player who gets results without creating enemies. The project manager who gets projects completed on time without alienating project members or other managers is praised for his or her teamwork. And the self-sacrificing individual contributor who does more than his or her share of the heavy lifting is described by the manager as an outstanding team player.

Unfortunately, being judged by others as a poor team player has a more powerful impact than being judged as a good team player. The impact, however, is negative. Performance appraisal systems that evaluate people on their personal characteristics and behaviors usually refer to "team play." To receive a low rating on this factor is tantamount to being excluded from promotion to supervisor or team leader. The same low rating on team play will disqualify a person from choice assignments such as representing the unit on an interdisciplinary team.

So far I have mentioned good team players and poor team players, following the logic of either-or thinking. In reality, the organizational world is more subtle. People who break away from the pack are outstanding team players. Yet they retain enough of their individuality to prevent them from totally sacrificing their welfare for the welfare of the group.

Like a tightrope walker, breakthrough team players carry out a delicate balancing act. They are recognized as strong team players, but do not capitulate so far to the team player side that their individual contribution is obscured. In this way break-through players position themselves for promotions, bonuses, choice assignments, and telephone calls from executive search firms. The team player who eventually pulls away from the others is unique in such talents as imagination, problem-solving ability, and leadership skills.

Take the accompanying self-quiz to help raise your awareness of the subtle difference between being a complete team loyalist and a solid team player who still achieves individual recognition.

Self-Quiz for Team Play Versus Individual Play

Indicate how you would most likely respond in the brief scenarios presented next by circling statement A or statement B.

1. During a staff meeting, a colleague presents a creative idea that is immediately accepted by the group. To your astonishment, his idea is exactly what you had in mind when it was your turn to present.

    A. I would congratulate the person who presented the idea and offer him total support. I wouldn't bother to mention that I had the same idea.

    B. I would congratulate the person who presented the idea and offer him my total support. I would then say something like, "What a coincidence, I have the same suggestion written down right here. However, I have an additional detail I would like to add."

2. You are part of a sales team located in Charlotte, North Carolina, that sells heavy equipment for the oil mining industry. It is mid-January, and you receive a phone call from the president of a major customer in Anchorage, Alaska. She demands that a company representative visit her company in three days to resolve a service problem or the contract with your company will be canceled. The members of the team sit in silence wondering how to respond.

    A. Sensing that here is an opportunity to be a corporate hero or heroine, you say to the group: "Although I'm not accustomed to an Alaskan winter, I volunteer to take care of this pressing customer need. I'll make flight arrangements within one hour. I'll report back to you by phone."

   B. You offer to fly up to Anchorage, providing that another team member can accompany you. You want the moral support, and besides you think such a big problem should be tackled as a team effort.

3. On your project team, members take turns making presentations to the group. The usual mode of presentation is to use flip charts, felt-tip pens, and pointers. On your own time you have learned how to use a computerized presentation package that enables you to make visually exciting presentations.

   A. You ask the project manager for fifteen minutes during the next meeting to describe your new skills. You suggest that other group members also learn how to make these high-tech presentations, and you volunteer to share your new expertise.

   B. For your next presentation you surprise and dazzle the group with your new computerized presentation package. After receiving "oohs and ahs" you volunteer to share your expertise with the other members of the project team.

4. Your company has a four-day work conference for managers scheduled at a warm-weather resort. Ample time is available for recreation, including a company tennis tournament organized by the resort staff. You are a seasoned tennis player with extensive tournament experience.

   A. You sign up immediately for the singles tournament, while silently licking your chops in anticipation of showcasing your talents to your colleagues. You also intend to enter the doubles division, but only after asking around to find a strong partner. You figure that with a strong partner, you would be a sure bet to win the company tournament.

   B. You ask if you can enter into the doubles tournament, and purposely select one of the weaker players to be your partner. During the tournament you play at a leisurely pace with an emphasis on trying to make your partner look good and not frustrating your opponents. You and your partner finish second, and you emphasize how much fun it was playing tennis with your colleagues.

5. Margot, the department assistant, has been performing above expectations ever since she joined your group two years ago. Holiday time is approaching and you are preparing your holiday gift list.

A. You suggest to your teammates that the team chip in to buy Margot a more expensive than average gift this year because of her exceptional performance.

B. You suggest to your teammates that the team chip in to buy Margot a more expensive than average gift this year because of her exceptional performance. In addition, you give Margot a cash gift in recognition of the outstanding work she has done for you.

6. You have been appointed to a task force to streamline (reengineer) work throughout the company. During the first meeting, the task force leader asks, "Who would like to be the note-taker today?"

A. Recognizing that here is a chance to gain valuable experience, you whisper to a less experienced member of the team and suggest that he take this opportunity.

B. Recognizing that here is a chance to gain valuable experience and to have your name prominently displayed, you volunteer to be the note-taker. You intend to do an outstanding job so you will be able to retain this role because of its opportunity for recognition.

7. The team has gathered to deal with a vital organizational problem, increasing the productivity of the group without hiring additional staff. You have known about this agenda for a week, and fortunately you find an article in *Management Review* that deals with the same problem.

A. You carefully study the article until you are entirely familiar with this new approach to increasing productivity within your group without increasing staff. During the meeting you explain this new approach and ask for the input of others concerning its applicability to your situation. The group, of course, is dependent on you for the details.

B. You carefully study the article until you are entirely familiar with this new approach to increasing productivity within your group without increasing staff. You make a photocopy of the article for each team member, and you include a note stating that you intend to introduce this idea during the upcoming meeting. During the meeting the article is discussed, and each member has a full understanding of the method. You contribute to the discussion but are not considered the resident expert on the topic.

8. You work with a group of information systems specialists. The team helps a small subsidiary install a complex inventory control system, and you serve as the contact person with the president. One month after the system is installed, the president of the subsidiary writes you a note expressing appreciation for the remarkable improvements you have made in her company's inventory management.

    A. You send the president a thank-you note, and also send a copy of her letter to your boss. You include an accompanying note explaining what a pleasure it is to work with an internal client of this type, and how well your team worked together.

    B. You send the president a thank-you note explaining that it was really your entire team that made the contribution. You therefore have all your teammates sign your letter to the president. You send a copy of the original letter plus your response with the co-signatures to your boss.

9. You are a member of a sales team that supplies fireproofing systems to manufacturing plants and offices. Business is doing well, partially because companies that install your systems can usually get their fire insurance premiums reduced. Today you are meeting for the second time with a small company that you consider to be ready to sign. Your boss asks you to bring along Randy, a new member of the sales team, so he can observe how to close a sale. During the meeting, you close the sale.

    A. After the sale, you compliment Randy on how attentive he was and thank him for contributing to the sale. When you return to the office, you tell the sales manager the same thing you told Randy about his contribution.

    B. As the sale is about to close, you ask Randy to present the contract to the customer and sign his name. After the sale, you congratulate Randy on making his first sale.

You explain that his career is off to a good start because
he has pinned down that all-important first sale. You explain to the sales manager that in your opinion Randy
should receive credit for the sale, as indicated by his sig-
nature on the contract.

10. You are a professional member of an advertising
agency. You pass by the office of Angela, a copywriter who is
deep in thought, just sitting at her Macintosh. Angela asks, "Do
you have a minute?" She then explains that she has reached a
mental block in trying to find an attention-grabbing slogan for
an advertising campaign promoting denture cream. You observe
that too many denture cream campaigns focus on worrying
about dentures coming loose while eating food or chewing gum.
You emphasize that other oral activities can also produce anxieties for denture wearers. An idea flashes in your mind. You suggest to Angela that she play with the slogan, KISS IN COMFORT.
"That's great, I owe you one," responds Angela.

   A. You walk away from Angela's office quite happy that you
      have helped a team member. You know that you will ex-
      perience a warm inner glow when you hear the phrase
      KISS IN COMFORT while watching a denture cream ad
      on television.
   B. You walk away from Angela's office quite happy that you
      have helped a team member. You will have the same
      warm glow experience as in statement A. You take your
      team contribution one step further, however. In stating
      your list of accomplishments in preparation for your an-
      nual review, you include the item: "On occasion, serve
      as resource person for helping other members of the
      staff with creative ideas."

Interpretation of Team Play Quiz

The purpose of this self-quiz is not primarily to see how high you
score on tendencies toward being a breakthrough team player.
Instead, I am more concerned about sensitizing you to capitaliz-
ing on opportunities to be a good team player, yet simultaneously squeezing individual recognition from the situation. The
ideal outcome from carefully following the information in this
book would be to become a person who helps the team, the

organization, and you to succeed. Such a person is the true breakthrough team player.

Scenario 1: "A" is the team player response. You are a good team player who is not particularly concerned about individual recognition.

"B" is the breakthrough team player response. You display good team play by congratulating the person who beat you to the punch. You also let it be known, however, that you are thinking along similar lines and that you would like to *make an additional contribution.*

Scenario 2: "A" is the breakthrough team player response. You volunteer to help the team in a challenging situation. If you resolve the service problem you will be remembered as a hero or heroine. If you fail, at least you tried, including inconveniencing yourself by braving a trip to Anchorage in mid-January. (You do not publicize the fact that Anchorage is much warmer in mid-January than most people from Charlotte, North Carolina, realize.) Besides, how often do you get an expense-paid trip to Alaska?

"B" is the team player response. You want to solve this demanding customer problem, and you think that two heads should prove to be better than one. Also, if two people make the trip, solving the problem will be more explicitly a team effort. If the two of you fail, at least you made a good team effort and will be recognized accordingly.

Scenario 3: "A" is the team player response. You introduce new technology to the group without particular concern for receiving individual recognition. Other team members will not be outdone by the way you have introduced the new technology.

"B" is the breakthrough team player response. The rest of the group will soon benefit from using high-tech presentations. Yet the element of surprise is effective. You will be remembered for having made the first dazzling presentation.

Scenario 4: Choosing between the breakthrough team player versus regular team player response in this scenario is difficult. The difference between the two is subtle. "A" is closer to the breakthrough team player response. You display team spirit because you participate in the tournament, and especially because you enter the doubles division also. Yet you will be remembered for your tennis skill, particularly because you won. Outstanding athletes can still maintain a team player reputation.

"B" is the team player response. You are so self-sacrificing that you do not walk away with a trophy. Yet you will receive credit for having good team spirit. The way you work with your partner shows exceptional team play, but you will not be remembered as a winner, which is a major contributor to entering the breakthrough category.

Scenario 5: "A" is the team player response. You are sensitive to the needs of Margot, an important team contributor. You also want to work cooperatively with the rest of the group in recognizing her accomplishments.

"B" is the breakthrough response. You work cooperatively with the rest of the team in recognizing Margot's accomplishments, but you also gain a few recognition points. Margot is likely to speak glowingly about you to your boss. Notice also that in both scenarios you have exercised leadership that will help you achieve breakthrough status.

Scenario 6: "A" is the team player response. You admirably share your wisdom with a less experienced team member to enhance his development. The person will probably remember your kindness.

"B" is the breakthrough team player response. The note-taker role is deceptively important. You can shape which points made in the meeting receive the most emphasis and become a permanent record. Your contribution will be remembered if your minutes are coherent and useful. Remember, the name of the person who took the minutes appears at the top of the memo. Key people will have an electronic or hard copy reminder of your contribution.

Scenario 7: "A" is the breakthrough team player response. You show that you are a good team player by bringing important information to the group's attention. Nevertheless, you exert control over the information because the others do not have immediate access to the material. You are regarded positively as a team player because you bring fresh ideas to the team's attention.

"B" is the team player response. You give teammates advance notice of your proposal so they can participate fully in the discussion, thus sharing the spotlight. In this situation being a regular team player might be more advantageous to the group than being a breakthrough player. With advance information about the new method of enhancing productivity, the team might be able to use it more effectively at the initial meeting. You usually will not face an ethical conflict by functioning as a breakthrough team player, because such an individual finds a way to benefit all. However, in this situation the breakthrough approach will delay full benefit to all until the next meeting, when the other team members have had an opportunity to study the article.

Scenario 8: "A" is the breakthrough team player response. You share credit with the team but also accept the individual recognition you deserve.

"B" is the team player response. You go out of your way to share credit with the team, perhaps at the expense of not receiving some of the credit you deserve.

Scenario 9: "A" is the breakthrough team player choice. You give Randy appropriate credit, while at the same time receiving the credit you deserve.

"B" is the team player choice. You go out of your way to boost Randy's morale, and give him undue credit for his contribution to the sale. In this situation, the breakthrough team player choice is the more ethical one. By choosing "B" your ethics appear shaky. You are crediting another member of the team with a sale to which he only made a minor contribution.

Scenario 10: "A" is the team player choice because you help a teammate with an important work problem with no specific concern about receiving credit yourself. Your reward is the good deed itself; you will experience an inner glow whenever you think of the slogan, KISS IN COMFORT.

"B" is the breakthrough team player choice. You still get all the psychic goodies you would have by choosing alternative A, but you also squeeze individual recognition out of the situation.

Letting the Glory Rub Off on You

A key principle underlying the breakthrough team player choices described above is that you should look for a way to let some of the team glory rub off on you. If you fail to do so, you may miss an opportunity for individual recognition. You can most readily apply this principle when you have been team leader.

Suppose you have been the leader of a committee or project that did an outstanding job, such as exceeding quality targets on product improvement. Suggest to the manager you report to on this project that the team should receive symbolic recognition. Perhaps the company will be willing to purchase a team plaque for each member. Summarize the team's accomplishment on the plaque, and have your name listed as team leader. Although a modest gain, this will be one more situation in which you distinguish yourself.

Figuring out how to let the glory rub off on you in a team situation is challenging. The group has to perform well on an important task, and you have to make a legitimate contribution to the effort. In addition, you have to tactfully inform somebody in authority of these accomplishments. Here are two techniques team leaders and team members can use to let the glory rub off on them.

Expressing Pride in the Group

Sara was assigned to a task force to improve her savings and loan association's method of processing home mortgages. Her institution required an average of six more days than competitors to process an application. Based on this delay, many real estate agents steered their clients to other mortgage lenders. Sara's task force dutifully studied the mortgage process and was able to shorten it by seven days. The task force discovered, for example, that the mortgage applications moved slowly from department to department, waiting each time for the department to accomplish its work.

Data were collected for one year after the new loan application process was implemented. The bank officers concluded that the ratio of mortgages granted to applications received had improved substantially. Sara, as well as other members of the task force, was informed of the favorable analysis.

Sara's responsibility to the task force now dwindled to about two hours per week to check on continued implementation of the new procedures. During a meeting with a senior vice president, the executive asked Sara how her work was going. Sara reported that she was experiencing a surge of pride these days. "What are you so proud of?" asked the senior vice president.

Sara responded, "I'm proud to be part of a task force that has done the bank so much good. Our mortgages completed to applications processed ratio is the best it's ever been. My contribution wasn't any greater than any other team member, yet I hope you will understand my feeling proud."

Six months later Sara received a promotion to assistant vice president. She feels that her discussion about the pride she experienced helped establish a favorable work relationship with the senior vice president. The same executive serves on the promotion committee of the bank.

Documenting Your Contribution to the Team

A problem with many team efforts from the standpoint of career advancement is that the team receives most of the credit for the work accomplished. If the team works as designed, with members contributing equally, giving the team most of the credit is correct. In many teams, however, one or two people make the major contributions while the others enjoy the ride—and the credit. The challenge then is to receive the credit you feel you deserve without appearing egotistical and anti-team. Finding a way to tactfully document your contribution to the team can help you cope with the problem of not receiving credit for an above-average contribution to the team.

Mark, a certified public accountant, found a way to document his contribution to a team whose work was central to the mission of his firm. Mark's firm was experiencing a business plateau. As more large business companies gobbled up smaller companies, the demand for accounting services decreased. (Fewer companies were available to hire accountants.) In addition, more companies were doing more of their accounting internally. Mark served on a client-development team that uncovered several productive ways of expanding the firm's practice. Among these thrusts was to advertise and hold tax seminars free to the public.

The team received ample credit from the senior partners for helping the practice grow. However, Mark believed that he deserved more credit than several of the other team members. Nevertheless he did not want to appear tacky by stating this observation to the senior partners. Instead, he cleverly wrote an e-mail message describing his contribution without asking for credit. His electronic message stated:

> Thanks for the opportunity to serve on the client development team. I'm pleased that the team accomplished its mission. My major assignment was to conduct tax seminars for the public. I found that to be a professionally rewarding experience. Should the opportunity arise to help the firm again by conducting seminars, please consider me as a candidate.

Mark's actions helped him achieve glory for two important reasons. First, he knew that the public seminars were successful and that his contribution to them would therefore be considered significant. Second, he did not ask for credit in his message. He simply stated that he enjoyed contributing to the firm by giving public seminars. A little modesty is helpful, especially in a conservative environment such as a CPA firm.

Knowing When to Make the Decision by Yourself

An effective team player by definition uses group decision making rather than individual decision making. Yet people are often promoted because they are imaginative and bold decision makers. Again, you have to walk the tightrope to become a breakthrough team player. You have to know when the time is right to make a decision by yourself and when to involve one or more team members.

A key factor in making a group decision is how much to involve other people. Using a consultative style, you merely collect input from others and then make your decision. An intermediate position is to fully discuss the situation to reach a consensus decision. The output is a decision each person in the group will support, even if they are not in total agreement. Using group involvement to the fullest, the group makes the decision democratically. Under this extreme form of group decision making, you might take a vote to reach a decision.

Choosing between individual and group decision making is a more obvious requirement when you are the team leader or manager. Yet individuals who are part of a team sometimes have the option of choosing between individual and group decision making. For example, a team member might decide to visit several suppliers without consulting others in the group.

Your goal is to make a good decision that brings credit to you and does not alienate others. Furthermore, you do not want to waste the team's time on a decision that could easily have been made by you. Following are guidelines, based on dozens of research studies and case histories, for choosing between making a decision by yourself and involving others in that decision. When faced with a consequential decision, answer the following questions:

1. *How important is the technical quality of this decision?* When the technical quality of a decision must be high, such as selecting the right software, it is important to involve knowledgeable teammates in the decision. Asking the opinion of uninformed or misinformed team members can lower the quality of the decision. A major pitfall of team-based organizations is that too many good-intentioned but unqualified people contribute to important decisions. How would you like to work in an office tower where many decisions about structural design were made by technically naive people just to placate employees who wanted to be empowered?

2. *How important is team member commitment to the decision?*
Typically, commitment is better when people are involved in
making the decision. Participative decision making thus offers a
political advantage. Yet most team members are unlikely to stay
committed to a bad decision, even if they were involved in making it. If an individual makes a unilateral decision that proves to
offer an important advantage to team members, commitment
will follow.

Several years back, many managers at J.C. Penney
were upset when the top merchandising executive decided to upgrade the company's line of clothing. The managers in question thought that J.C. Penney would lose its
traditional market and blur its customer focus. To the con-
trary, J.C. Penney has done remarkably well. As profit improvements brought along increases in compensation, the
dissidents became committed to the decision of upgrading
merchandise.

3. *If you made the decision by yourself, would other team members be committed to the decision?* The previous question asked
about the importance of commitment; this question asks about
the probability of commitment. If commitment is important,
choose between individual and group decision making on the
basis of which approach will most likely lead to commitment.
Because it is difficult to predict commitment, take the safe route
here and use group decision making if commitment is important.

4. *Do you have sufficient information to make a high-quality decision?* If you need more information, definitely consult with the
group. Emphasize input from the best-informed team members.
A key advantage of group decision making is that somebody
will catch a potential blooper. If your goal is to be a breakthrough team player, you want to avoid damaging your reputation by making low-quality decisions based on insufficient
information.

5. *Is the problem well defined?* If the problem is clear-cut (or
well structured) there is less need for group decision making. In

contrast, when the problem has many nuances, involving others in the decision increases in importance. An example of a well-defined problem would be whether to change suppliers on a commodity such as heating oil. An example of a problem with many nuances would be whether to modify the retirement medical benefits. Considerable emotion is involved in the latter decision, as well as the possibility of bad press if an unpopular decision is made.

6. *Do team members share the organizational goals to be attained in solving the problem?* If you think that the group cares about the organizational goal at issue in solving the problem, then involve the group. A classic case here is whether to involve team members in a work-streamlining program designed to eliminate several positions in the group. Teams members are typically opposed to an organizational goal of eliminating several of their jobs, so they should not be involved in making the decision. Later on, however, they can be involved in suggesting how to implement the decision.

7. *Is there conflict among team members over which solution is best?* If you think the team members will haggle over the solution chosen, it is best to involve them in making the decision. A team leader in a sales organization ordered six laptop computers for team members. Much to her surprise, the group argued about whether they should be required to learn how to use the machines. The team members with more computer knowledge argued about whether the most appropriate laptop computers were purchased. A veteran sales representative, for example, said the screen on his laptop was too small to read.

8. *Do team members have sufficient information to make a high-quality decision?* If team members have enough information to make a high-quality decision, they should be involved. If they lack such information, they should not be involved in making the decision. A breakthrough team player might supply the team with enough information so the members can make an effective decision.

9. *Are team members involved in a decision that you have already made?* Your credibility as a team leader or team player will diminish if you hold meetings about a decision that has already

been made. Such a meeting is perceived as subterfuge. A better alternative is to announce that the decision is already made but suggestions for implementation are invited. Returning to the laptop example, the team leader might have called a meeting to discuss how to make best use of the new machines that the company had generously allocated to them.[1]

When implementing the guidelines just presented, you may not have definitive answers for all nine. Run with the answers you do have, and look for the strongest trend. Suppose that you are confident of your answers to seven of the above questions, and that five of these seven favor involving the group. You would then involve the team in making the decision. Another consideration is that one of the above questions might be of overwhelming importance. Your response to that question would then override others. For example, in many decision-making situations, question 4 about your having sufficient information is critical. If you cannot make a high-quality decision by yourself, involve the group. Answers to other questions that point toward making the decision by yourself are of secondary importance.

Avoiding the Trap of Poor Team Play

In the quest to obtain individual recognition, some people fall into the self-defeating trap of being a poor team player. To be accused of being a poor team player is to be seen as a misfit, particularly in a bureaucracy. If your goal is to be a breakthrough team player, you must reflect on all your actions and anticipated actions to evaluate whether they might be interpreted as poor team play by key people. The situation of Conrad illustrates how being a poor team player yet still a fine performer can sabotage a person's career.

After graduating from college as an accounting major, Conrad fulfilled his ROTC obligation of two years of active

1. Based on information in Victor H. Vroom and Arthur G. Jago, *The New Leadership: Managing Participation in Organizations* (Englewood Cliffs, N.J.: Prentice-Hall, 1988).

duty as a military officer. He had a lot of respect for the army and the caliber of officers with whom he worked. Yet Conrad felt he was not well suited for a career in the military. In his words, "I'm too independent. I like to make decisions on my own. I need more flexibility and space than the army can provide. I would be better off in business or industry."

Conrad's next career move was to obtain a position with a CPA firm in Boston as a staff accountant. While in the army Conrad prepared for his CPA exam. Within eighteen months of working as a civilian, he passed all five parts of the exam. Conrad believed that his career opportunities were unlimited. His credentials were excellent, and his two years as an army lieutenant give him more leadership experience than his competitors had.

Conrad went about his work diligently, rarely having lunch or after-hours drinks with the other accountants. He reasoned that he was more serious-minded than his coworkers. Conrad was intent on becoming the highest producer in his unit. He succeeded, attaining the highest number of billable hours among the junior accountants in his office.

When a supervising position was created in Conrad's area, he was not chosen. Instead, the partners promoted a woman a little older than Conrad whose productivity was about average. Conrad was both perturbed and perplexed. Why would partners not choose him for supervisor when he was the highest producer in the office and an experienced leader to boot? At Conrad's request, the managing partner of the office explained why. Conrad was indeed a competent and productive accountant, but he was too much of a loner. He acted as if he were in business for himself instead of working as a member of the firm.

My key point so far is that the breakthrough team player maintains the delicate balance between being an excellent team player yet still receiving recognition for being an outstanding individual performer. The rest of the book will provide you with more information on how to accomplish this feat. Most books about success, your own education and training, and the advice of your mentors have dealt with being an outstanding individual performer. My intention therefore is to concentrate on the subtleties necessary to be an outstanding team player, yet leave room for eventually breaking away from the pack.

2

The Consummate Team Player

Breakthrough team players distinguish themselves from other team members. At the same time, they are highly effective, valued members of the team. Team play is important for obvious reasons. Without effective team players, the team structure cannot operate well. Being an effective team player is also important because of managerial perceptions.

A survey of fifteen business organizations in thirty-four industries indicates that employers rate "team player" as the most highly ranked workplace behavior. The study was conducted by Challenger, Gray & Christmas, Inc., an international outplacement firm. Approximately 40 percent of the managers surveyed ranked "team player" as number one among seven desirable traits. Furthermore, 80 percent of those surveyed rated "team player" as either first, second, or third on their list of desirable attributes.[1]

The purpose of this chapter is to help you enhance your effectiveness as a team player by describing the skills, actions, and attitudes required to be a consummate team player. You can regard these behaviors as goals for personal improvement. Identify the actions and attitudes where you need the most improvement, and proceed accordingly with self-development. Quite often you will be able to achieve the development you want through conscious effort and self-discipline. Self-development

1. " 'Team Player' Gets Top Spot in Survey" (undated sample copy distributed by Dartnell Corporation, 1994), p. 3.

can also be achieved through appropriate reading, seminars, videos, and audiocassettes.

A Ladder of Team Player Skills, Knowledge, and Attitudes

Similar to many industrial companies, the Eastman Kodak Company has created team structures throughout its operations. Teamwork is so important that Kodak has developed a ladder of team player skills, knowledge, and attitudes to guide newcomers and established employers. Although Kodak designed this ladder to inform and enlighten entry-level workers, it applies to team players at all levels.

Starting at the bottom of the ladder are basic team player skills, knowledge, and attitudes. At the top of the ladder are teamwork competencies required of outstanding team players. The competitive employee has most of the skills, knowledge, and attitudes indicated at the top of the ladder. Use the accompanying ladder of competencies as personal development suggestions toward becoming the consummate team player.

A Ladder of Skills, Knowledge, and Attitudes for Teamwork

Directions: In the right column, circle the letter that indicates whether you have that competence now (N) or it is an area for personal improvement (I).

Skill, Knowledge, or Attitude	Competency Level	
1. Attends team meetings regularly	N	I
2. Participates in team brainstorming	N	I
3. Works effectively as a team member by:		
• Sharing communication	N	I
• Negotiating	N	I
• Facilitating	N	I
• Participating	N	I
• Cooperating	N	I
• Trusting	N	I

Skill, Knowledge, or Attitude	*Competency Level*	
• Working toward and accepting consensus	N	I
• Functioning as a teacher and learner	N	I
• Valuing and using leadership skills	N	I
• Using conflict resolution skills	N	I
4. Makes original contributions to team issues; builds upon others' contributions	N	I
5. Volunteers to handle action items or to participate in new teams	N	I
6. Actively participates in establishing team's purpose, direction, strategy, or goals	N	I
7. Positively questions and challenges others; utilizes conflicting views in a constructive manner	N	I
8. Acts to create and promote team cohesiveness	N	I
9. Offers to relieve a team member's heavy workload	N	I
10. Considers impact on external interfaces when influencing team outcomes	N	I

Qualities Needed for Effective Team Play

Education, training, and coaching will help you move toward becoming the consummate team player. Yet you will need both self-discipline and self-empowerment to convert such knowledge into action. Effective team players guide their own behavior without requiring much inspiration or cajoling from the team leader or manager. Self-discipline and self-empowerment are important enough to examine separately.

Self-Discipline

In the present context, *self-discipline* is mobilizing one's energy and effort to stay focused on attaining an important goal. The outstanding team player pays unswerving attention to team goals and the tasks he or she must accomplish to achieve those goals. The poor team player often believes that taking it easy is okay because another team member can pick up the slack.

Susan A. Rabin is the CEO of a small gear-manufacturer located in Hamilton, Ontario. As she sees it, self-discipline is a major contributor to team effectiveness. Simpson notes that unless each member sticks to what needs to be accomplished, team productivity will suffer. In her words:

> Self-discipline is especially important when people are working as a team. A really enthusiastic attitude toward getting things done is contagious. Employees sitting around waiting for orders for everything waste a lot of productive time. Give an employee freedom to be creative, and let him know that you are confident that he will get the job done efficiently. The employee will then be determined to work productively and contribute to the team.

Self-Empowerment

Empowerment has become a buzzword in the modern organization. It generally refers to the process whereby people with more formal authority give part of their power to people with less formal authority. An empowered team is a work group that has the authority to conduct many of the activities that were formerly the province of managers. Being granted more power from a higher-ranking person often boosts morale and productivity. Although the consummate team player welcomes empowerment, he or she does not require it to perform well. Instead he or she practices *self-empowerment*—liberating yourself by assuming you have the authority to accomplish worthwhile ends.

A self-empowered team player recognizes problems and opportunities and then solves the problem or capitalizes upon the opportunity without first checking his or her job description.

Bill, a member of a customer service team in a gas and electric company, practiced self-empowerment. The mission of his team was to become a high-performing customer service operation by providing outstanding customer service to every external customer seeking assistance.

After working as a member of the customer service team for one year, Bill recognized the team was amiss in one important dimension of providing outstanding customer service. Approximately 10 percent of the customers who came to the office or telephoned understood Spanish much better than English. Yet only one member of the customer service team spoke Spanish fluently. Bill took it upon himself to recommend a combination of tapes and classroom instruction to help each member of the team master Spanish. The team leader and the other teammates agreed that developing competency in Spanish was long overdue. (Notice that the implementation of Bill's suggestion helped the team accomplish its mission and positioned him to achieve individual recognition.)

Bill's initiative is one example of how self-empowerment can help a person achieve outstanding team play. Here are two additional ways of practicing self-empowerment:

1. For years you have been waiting for the company to purchase a new software package and train you on its application. You are convinced this software will enhance your productivity. One day you recognize that it is time to empower yourself to learn this new software. You purchase the software with your own money, load it into your PC at home, and begin learning. Your investment in your own development quickly pays dividends as you begin to use this software to improve your productivity as a team member. (You hope that this productivity boost will eventually lead to a bigger bonus for yourself and the team.)

2. You have been waiting several years to be promoted to team leader so you can obtain some valuable leadership experience. Tired of waiting to receive the nod for a formal leadership assignment, you ask the team leader if you can take a few turns at running the team meeting. She obliges, and your act of self-empowerment has worked.

Task-Related Actions and Attitudes

Hundreds of different activities transpire while a team conducts its work. At one moment the group is silent while thinking analytically about a member's suggestion. At another moment someone says, "Let's break for ten minutes," and the activity stops. At another time the team leader turns on his laser spotlight to highlight a point on a flip chart. At still another moment a team member challenges the group by saying, "How does what we are doing right now support our mission?"

One convenient method for classifying team activities in pursuit of goals is task-related versus people-related. We begin first with the task-related actions and attitudes that contribute to outstanding team play. Remember, however, that the dichotomy of task- versus people-related activities lacks 100 percent accuracy. For example, if you are challenging your teammates with a difficult goal, are you focusing more on the task (achieving the goal) or the people (offering them a motivational challenge)?

Technical Expertise

Most people are chosen to join a particular work team on the basis of their technical expertise. By *technical* I refer to the intimate details of any task, not just tasks in engineering, physical science, and information technology. The sales promotion specialist on a product development team has technical expertise in sales promotion, whether or not sales promotion requires knowledge of engineering or computers.

As team consultant Glenn Parker observes, to use your technical expertise to outstanding advantage in a team effort, you must have the willingness and ability to share that expertise.[2] Some experts perceive their esoteric knowledge as a source of power. As a consequence, they are hesitant to let others share their knowledge for fear of relinquishing power.

According to Parker, it is also necessary for the technical

2. Glenn M. Parker, *Cross-Functional Teams: Working With Allies, Enemies & Other Strangers* (San Francisco: Jossey-Bass Publishers, 1994), p. 170.

expert to be able to communicate with team members in other disciplines who lack the same technical background. The technical person who cannot explain the potential value of his or her contribution may not receive much attention.

Helen was appointed as the information technology expert on a reengineering team. During the first several meetings of a reengineering team, Helen would periodically makes statements such as, "We can get this done in no time with IT (information technology)," or "It's just a question of replacing that function with the right technology."

When asked by teammates to explain specifically how information technology would do the job, Helen would say something like, "This would be difficult to explain to someone outside of information technology."

Helen was really asking the group to blindly accept her pronouncement that she could use information technology to accomplish most of the work simplification. Her refusal (or inability) to explain the specifics of her proposal lessened her potential contribution to the group. The other teammates were not buying what could not be explained.

Assuming Responsibility for Problems

The consummate team player assumes responsibility for problems. If a problem is free floating (not yet assigned to a specific person), he or she says, "I'll do it." One team member might remark that true progress on the team's effort will be blocked until the team benchmarks with other successful teams. The effective team player might volunteer, "You are right, we need to benchmark. If it's okay with everybody else, I'll get started on the benchmarking project tomorrow. It will be my responsibility."

The five magic words *It will be my responsibility* are golden to the team leader and other team members. They now know that this important chunk of the work will be done. If the person does a satisfactory job of benchmarking, other group members will be happy for him or her to handle other unassigned tasks in the future. Taking responsibility must therefore be combined with dependability. The person who takes responsibility for a task must produce time after time. A team member at a Xerox Corp. manufacturing plant explains the importance of responsibility and dependability:

> We have a spirit of kinship working in our Team Xerox unit. Anyone who lets us down is regarded as a poor team player. It would be the same as if a member of a basketball team decided to goof off on the night of an important game.

Willingness to Commit to Team Goals

Every team I have personally observed, read about, or heard about has explicit or implicit goals. At the same time, the individual team members may have goals of their own that may not overlap entirely with group goals. A gap between team goals and individual goals sometimes occurs within a cross-functional team. The team wants to achieve a multidisciplinary purpose such as developing a new product or reducing costs. The individual may have a few personal goals. One goal might be influencing the output of the group so the individual's functional department prospers. If, for example, the product development team develops a product with a heavy engineering component, the engineering representative on the team will be satisfied. At times the team member will also have a career goal. He or she is serving on the team primarily as a vehicle for gaining visibility.

The consummate team player will commit to team goals even if his or her personal goals cannot be achieved for now. The engineering representative on the cross-functional team will commit to producing a new product even if it will have a small engineering component. The team member seeking visibility will be enthusiastic about pursuing team goals even if not much visibility will be gained.

Ability to See the Big Picture

A basic management skill is to think conceptually, having the ability to see the big picture. Consummate team players should have the same skill. In team efforts discussion can get bogged down in small details, and the team might temporarily lose sight of what it is trying to accomplish.[3] The team player (or team leader) who can help the group focus on its broader purpose plays a vital role.

A sales-process-improvement team was asked to make it easier for customers to purchase office equipment when they visited the company's retail store. With the current process, five different people had to handle each sales transaction. The customer was often kept waiting for up to an hour. During the second session, the group began to vent their hostility toward the warehouse specialists. As the conversation became more heated, several of the team members discussed documenting all the problems created by the warehouse specialists and then reporting them to the vice president of marketing. As emotions intensified, several team members began to ridicule the warehouse workers.

Beth, the store manager and one of the team members, helped the group step back and see the big picture. She challenged the group in these words: "Hold on, why are we here? Is our purpose to improve the sales process or to castigate the very people who keep in stock something for us to sell." The team accepted the confrontation and praised Beth for her contribution. [*Beth is following one of the basic tenets of the breakthrough team player. She is making an outstanding contribution to the group while simultaneously distinguishing herself.*]

Belief in Consensus

A major task-related attitude for outstanding team play is to genuinely believe that consensus has merit. Consensus is general acceptance by the group of a decision. All team members may not be thrilled about the decision, but they are not opposed to it. Equally important, they are willing to live with and support the decision.

3. Ibid.

Believing that consensus is a workable philosophy enables you to participate fully in team decisions without thinking that you have sacrificed your beliefs or the right to think independently. To believe in consensus is to believe that the democratic process has relevance for organizations, and that ideal solutions are not always possible.

The consensus attitude required is similar to that required by the losing politician in a contest for the party nomination. While campaigning for the position, the candidates may express divergent views and perhaps trade insults. Yet the politician who fails to get the candidacy will make a public statement that he or she is fully behind the winning candidate. This display of team solidarity is good for the party. Similarly, the team player who has an opposing position should be willing to embrace the final decision. To do so marks him or her as a good team player. A disgruntled heel dragger is a poor team player.

Willingness to Ask Tough Questions

The consummate team player is not a sycophant who avoids challenging the group's thinking for fear of being disliked by the team leader or other members. A major contribution of asking tough questions is that it helps the group avoid the dysfunctional type of consensus called *groupthink*. This occurs when group members become so caught up in attempting to achieve cohesiveness and camaraderie that they avoid mutual criticism. In the sales-process-improvement team situation described earlier, the group nearly made the poor decision of documenting all the mistakes of the warehouse specialists.

A *tough question* helps the group achieve insight into the nature of the problem it is facing, what it might be doing wrong, and whether progress is sufficient. Tough questions can also be asked to help the group see the big picture. Here are two tough question scenarios:

1. A production work team has met six times to design the work layout for assembling a giant-screen television receiver. One member of the group says, "I've been to all

our meetings so far. What in heaven's name have we accomplished?"
2. A top management team is in the middle of a weekend retreat to analyze how to restructure the company. One member of the executive team says, "I've listened to us bat this issue around for ten hours. So far all I've heard about is the slash-and-burn perspective. When are we going to start talking about positive thrusts like developing new products and opening new markets?"

Helping Team Members Do Their Jobs Better

Your stature as a team player will increase if you take the initiative to help coworkers make needed work improvements. Helping other team members with their work assignments is a high-level form of cooperation. Make the suggestions in a constructive spirit instead of displaying an air of superiority.

Priscilla, a software engineer, suggested to her team members that they make their overview charts more exciting, adding a logo, producing the charts in color, and being more creative in general. The change dramatically improved presentations to user groups. People stayed more alert and interested during briefings. Priscilla received many words of appreciation for her dedication to the group cause.

Lending a Hand During Peak Workloads

A natural opportunity for being a good team player arises during peak workloads. If you have any slack time, volunteer to help a teammate who is overloaded. Even an hour or two of assistance to take some pressure off a coworker will strengthen your role as a team player. Your psychological costs in using this technique can be reduced if you help out on activities you can easily handle. For example, if you are adept at compiling data for reports, stand ready to help an overloaded team member with statistics gathering.

Rarely Turning Down a Coworker Request

Granting requests for help from coworkers is governed by the theory of reinforcement. If you comply with a request from a coworker, he or she will be rewarded and return with another request. If you turn down more than a couple of requests, that coworker will stop making requests. If you want to be left alone, just turn down a few requests. If you want to be perceived as a team player, however, accept any reasonable request. In a smooth-functioning team, members routinely honor requests from each other. Should you not be able or willing to handle a request from a coworker, turn it down diplomatically.

Grant, a hospital administrator, characteristically grants requests from coworkers to do such things as review their reports and budgets. When he doesn't have the time, Grant finds a way to turn down the request diplomatically. One of his most effective ways of turning down a request gently is to say, "I wish I could help you right now. Yet with my current workload, I won't be able to get to your project until Sunday afternoon." [*Notice how guilty the mention of Sunday afternoon probably made the coworker feel.*] Using this hedge, Grant will be remembered as willing to help. Because Grant uses this stalling technique only occasionally, it is effective.

Openness to New Ideas

A key characteristic of an effective work team is that members think freely and creatively. Thinking freely and creatively can only be effective if people are willing to listen to and consider the ideas of others even when these ideas conflict with their own. As organizations continue to emphasize multidisciplinary teams, more groups will harbor differing ideas. Being open to new ideas is therefore increasing in importance as an attitude characteristic of breakthrough team players.

Engaging in Mutually Beneficial Exchanges

An effective team player regularly exchanges favors with coworkers. You explicitly or implicitly promise that the other person will benefit later if he or she complies with your request. A more coercive way to use exchange is to remind the coworker that he or she *owes you one*. A spirit of teamwork develops as group members engage in mutually beneficial exchanges. Here are a few workplace exchanges that can foster teamwork:

- You agree to take care of an angry customer because one of your coworkers is too stressed today to absorb one more hassle.
- You cover for a team member who needs a few hours off to speak to her estate planner.
- You agree to attend the Little League soccer game of a coworker's son, providing he will attend one of your daughter's soccer games.
- You help a team member prepare an overdue report, recognizing that you are now owed a favor.

Engaging in mutually beneficial exchanges can be either task- or people-related, depending upon the nature of the favor. The exchange tactic can thus be used to facilitate accomplishment of the team's work directly or to build relationships within the group.

Before moving on to the people-related actions and attitudes of the consummate team player, pause to review the accompanying list of what has just been covered.

Task-Related Actions and Attitudes

- Technical expertise
- Assuming responsibility for problems
- Willingness to commit to team goals
- Ability to see the big picture
- Belief in consensus
- Willingness to ask tough questions
- Helping team members do their jobs better
- Lending a hand during peak workloads
- Rarely turning down a coworker request
- Openness to new ideas
- Engaging in mutually beneficial exchanges

People-Related Actions and Attitudes

Consummate team players are consciously aware of their interpersonal relations within the group. They recognize that effective interpersonal relationships are important for getting tasks accomplished. At the same time they are aware that interpersonal relationships are meaningless if they do not contribute to task accomplishment.

Trusting Team Members

The cornerstone attitude of the outstanding team player is to trust team members. Working on a team is akin to a small-business partnership. If you do not believe that the other team members have your best interests at heart, it will be difficult to share opinions and ideas. You will fear being backstabbed and badmouthed. (Not to say that this *never* happens in the team-based organization.)

Trusting team members includes believing that their ideas are technically sound and rational until proven otherwise. Another manifestation of trust is taking risk with others. You can take a risk by trying out a team member's unproven ideas. You can also take a risk by submitting an unproven idea without worrying about being ridiculed.

These are a couple of key meanings of trust, yet *trust* is an abstract concept with many subjective interpretations. Brent, a mechanical engineer, gives his idiosyncratic meaning of trust:

> I serve on an interdisciplinary team concerned with launching new products. To me trust means that I can be absent from a meeting without worrying that the team will make a decision that circumvents my point of view. In the previous division where I worked, I was afraid to ever miss a meeting. The prevailing attitude was, Now we no longer have to worry about trying to please the demands of mechanical engineering.

Sharing the Glory

A not-to-be overlooked tactic for emphasizing teamwork is to share credit for your accomplishments with the team. Glory sharing is not just a manipulative ploy. If you work in a team setting, other members of the team usually have contributed to the success of a product.

> Jerry, a production manager, was recognized at a company meeting for reducing the production cost of a critical component by 32 percent. Though Jerry originated the productivity-improvement idea, he immediately mentioned several engineers and production technicians who assisted him. By acknowledging the contribution of other workers, Jerry improved his status as a team player. Later that day a production engineer within the group gave Jerry a handshake of appreciation.

Recognizing the Interests and Achievements of Others

Back to Human Relations 101 and Dale Carnegie: A fundamental tactic for establishing yourself as a solid team player is to recognize actively the interests and achievements of others. Let others know that you care about their interests. After you make a suggestion during a team meeting, ask "Would my suggestion create any problems for anybody else?" or "How do my ideas fit into what you have planned?"

Recognizing the achievements of others is more straightforward than recognizing their interests. Be prepared to compliment any tangible achievement. Give realistic compliments by making the compliment commensurate with the achievement. To do otherwise is to compromise the sincerity of your compliment.

> During one meeting, financial analyst Elizabeth presented a spreadsheet analysis of how many years it would take to recoup several energy-saving suggestions. Jason, one of her teammates, responded, "Thanks Elizabeth,

that's the most concrete analysis of return on investment I've seen. Great input and much appreciated."

Elizabeth felt proud in response to a compliment of this magnitude. Jason would have wasted the opportunity for relationship building if he had said, "Incredible. Never before have I seen such a brilliant display of financial analysis." Elizabeth would have doubted his sincerity.

High Level of Cooperation and Collaboration

Cooperation and collaboration are synonymous with teamwork. If you display a willingness to help others and work cooperatively with them, you will be regarded as a team player. If you do not cooperate with other members of the team, the team structure breaks down. Collaboration at a team level means working jointly with others to solve mutual problems. Although working with another person on a given problem may take longer than working through a problem yourself, the long-term payout is important. You have established a climate favorable to working on joint problems where collective action is necessary.

Achieving a cooperative team spirit is often a question of making the first move. Instead of grumbling about poor teamwork, take the initiative and launch an atmosphere of cooperation in your group. Target the most individualistic, least cooperative member of the group. Ask the person for his or her input on an idea you are formulating. Thank the person, then state that you would be privileged to return the favor.

Active Listening and Information Sharing

The skilled team player is an active listener in the true sense of the term. An active listener strives to grasp both the facts of and the feelings behind what is being said. Observing the teammate's nonverbal communication is another part of active listening. For example, listen to the team member's tone of voice to see if there is emotion behind what is being said. Is this person really committed to a course of action (as indicated by his emotional state), or is he just releasing a trial balloon?

As part of active listening, you might also offer the other

person brief summary statements of your interpretation of what is being said. One example: "What you are telling the team is that the implementation of our proposal will not be cost effective."

While active listening reflects a high level of message reception, information sharing reflects a level of messages sent. Information sharing helps other team members do their job well and also communicates concern for their welfare. Information sharing can take such forms as bringing in news clips, magazine articles, and printouts from retrieval services, and recommending relevant books. Passing along rumors of a positive nature is another potentially effective form of information sharing.

Giving Helpful Criticism

The consummate team player offers constructive criticism when needed, but does so diplomatically. To do otherwise is to let the team down. A high-performance team demands sincere and tactful criticism between members. No matter how diplomatic you are, keep your ratio of criticism to praise small. This book is not the place for a brief treatise on constructive criticism, but keep two time-tested principles in mind.

1. Attempt to criticize the person's work or idea, not the person. It is better to say, "The conclusion is missing from your analysis," than "You left out the conclusion." (The latter statement hurts more because it sounds like your teammate did something wrong.)

2. A less well-known guideline for criticism is to ask a question rather than make a declarative statement. By answering a question the person being criticized is involved in improving his or her work. In the example at hand it would be effective to ask, "Do you think your report would have a bigger impact if it contained a conclusion?" In this way, the person being criticized contributes a judgment. The person has a chance to say, "Yes, I will prepare a conclusion."

Receptiveness to Helpful Criticism

In addition to criticizing others in a helpful manner, the consummate team player benefits from criticism directed toward him or her. A high-performing team involves much give and take including criticism of each other's ideas. The willingness to accept constructive criticism is often referred to as *self-awareness*. The self-aware team player insightfully processes personal feedback to improve effectiveness.

A team leader might observe that three key group members left her group over a six-month time span. (Team members leaving the group is an indirect form of feedback.) She might defensively dismiss this fact with an analysis such as, "I guess we just don't pay well enough to keep good people." The leader's first analysis might be correct. With a self-awareness orientation, however, the leader would dig deeper for the reasons behind the turnover. She might ask herself, "Is there something in my leadership approach that creates turnover problems?" She might ask for exit-interview data to sharpen her perceptions about her leadership approach.

Giving the Benefit of the Doubt

The effective team player criticizes and confronts when necessary, but remains flexible. He or she is often willing to take a teammate's word rather than engage in needless disputes. A teammate, for example, might bring data to a meeting. After poring over the material, you are intuitively concerned about its authenticity. You lack hard evidence that the data are weak. So instead of confronting your teammate, you accept the input. Perhaps the next time you will not be so generous, but for now you give your teammate the benefit of the doubt.

Being a Team Player Even When
Personally Inconvenienced

Another effective teamwork behavior is to do what is best for the team even if it causes you an inconvenience. This small bit of self-sacrifice may help build your reputation as an outstanding team player. Frequently in today's understaffed workplace team meetings are held at inconvenient hours, such as before or after normal working hours. For many parents with young children and others with major personal obligations, these meetings are grossly inconvenient.

Your reputation as a team player will suffer if you complain vehemently about these inconvenient meetings. Instead, it is better to develop back-up support people who can pinch-hit for you on last-minute schedule changes. Each person, however, has to decide upon limits to personal inconvenience he or she is willing to withstand. At some point your reputation as a reliable family member becomes more important than your reputation as a reliable team member.

Keeping Up the Team Spirit When Things Are Going Poorly

A final method for being a consummate team player is to take on the role of a motivator when the team hits a snag. Help keep the group focused on possible favorable outcomes even if the situation appears bleak.

Tammy was a copywriter at an advertising agency that was hard hit by a decline in client advertising. Her message to the group was that advertising always runs in cycles. Tammy also noted that the bottom point had already been reached.

Tammy encouraged the team by reminding them that management was attempting to increase advertising activity outside the usual channels. Tammy proved to be right. The company soon landed a few big contracts to conduct direct mail advertising. The payout to Tammy was that team spirit did not deteriorate, and two colleagues told Tammy they appreciated her support.

As a quick review of people-related actions and attitudes of the consummate team player, scan the following list.

People-Related Actions and Attitudes

- Trusting team members
- Sharing the glory

- Recognizing the interests and achievements of others
- High level of cooperation and collaboration
- Active listening and information sharing
- Giving helpful criticism
- Receptiveness to helpful criticism
- Giving the benefit of the doubt
- Being a team player even when personally inconvenienced
- Keeping up the team spirit when things are going poorly

Now that you have developed a clear picture of what it takes to be a consummate team player, the next chapter deals with the problem of going too far to be like others.

3

Avoiding the Conformity Trap

How do breakthrough players avoid thinking and acting like other members of the team while still remaining effective team players? Breakthrough team players value teamwork, yet recognize that the individual is still the most important unit within the organization. Organization development consultant Stanley M. Herman puts it this way: "All human organizations, no matter how simple or complex, large or small, are based on interaction between individuals. Therefore, a crucial element of the success or failure of an enterprise depends on the results of interaction between key individuals."[1]

Conformity is thinking and acting similarly to other group members in response to real or imagined pressure. The new team member learns quickly through being told or by observation that certain behaviors and thoughts are welcome while others are not. Conformity is not always a conscious decision. Without realizing it the group member begins to act and think like the others. The person may initially have a conflict with group norms, but resolves this conflict by acting like the others. Assume, for example, that other people in the group believe strongly that their company has a world-class product line. The newcomer to the group may not see it that way. Yet rather than enter into conflict with the group over this issue, he begins to perceive the products to be world-class. The organization loses

1. Stanley M. Herman, *A Force of Ones: Reclaiming Individual Power in a Time of Teams, Work Groups, and Other Crowds* (San Francisco: Jossey-Bass Publishers, 1994), p. 1.

out because conformity of this type blocks critical thinking that might lead to improved products.

As a starting point in scrutinizing the conformity trap, do the accompanying quiz. It is designed to give you tentative insight into your tendencies toward conformity. At the same time the quiz will sensitize you to many of the actions and thoughts involved in conformity.

The Conformity Quiz

Directions: Indicate on the following scale the extent to which each of the following statements describes your behavior or attitude: agree strongly (AS); agree (A); neutral (N); disagree (D); disagree strongly (DS). Circle the most accurate answer. Consider having someone who is familiar with your behavior and attitudes help you respond accurately.

	AS	A	N	D	DS
1. I rarely question the decision reached by the team.	5	4	3	2	1
2. Whatever the group wants is fine with me.	5	4	3	2	1
3. My clothing distinguishes me from the other members of the team.	1	2	3	4	5
4. I consider myself to be one of the office gang.	5	4	3	2	1
5. I rarely express disagreement during a group discussion.	5	4	3	2	1
6. I routinely have lunch with other members of my team.	5	4	3	2	1
7. My teammates sometimes complain that I think too independently.	1	2	3	4	5
8. My preference is to piggyback on the ideas of others rather than contribute ideas of my own.	5	4	3	2	1
9. When I notice that other members of the team make the same error in speech, I will copy					

	AS	A	N	D	DS
them rather than sound different.	5	4	3	2	1
10. I am often the first person to get up at the scheduled ending time of the meeting.	1	2	3	4	5
11. I do almost all of my creative thinking for the job when I'm with the team.	5	4	3	2	1
12. I'm particularly careful not to criticize an idea submitted by the team leader.	5	4	3	2	1
13. The number of hours I work per week corresponds closely to the number worked by my teammates.	5	4	3	2	1
14. When I think it is necessary, I bring information to the group that conflicts with the path we are following.	1	2	3	4	5
15. I would rather bite my tongue than point out weaknesses in a teammate's ideas.	5	4	3	2	1
16. I've been called a maverick on more than one occasion by teammates.	1	2	3	4	5
17. I encourage team members to express doubts about proposed solutions to problems.	1	2	3	4	5
18. I invite criticism of my ideas.	1	2	3	4	5
19. When the team laughs at a comment, I laugh too, even if I don't think the comment was funny.	5	4	3	2	1
20. Most of my social life centers around activities with my teammates.	5	4	3	2	1

Scoring and interpretation: Calculate your score by adding the numbers circled, and use the following scoring guide:

80–100   You are a highly conforming individual who readily goes along with the team without preserving your individuality. In an effort to be liked, you might be overcompromising your own thinking.

40–79   You have probably achieved the right balance between following group norms and expressing your individuality. With actions and attitudes like this, you are on your way to becoming a breakthrough team player.

20–29   You are highly individualistic, perhaps to the point of not working smoothly in a group setting. Be careful that you are not going out of your way to be a nonconformist, thereby interfering with your ability to be an effective team player.

Analysis of Conforming Actions and Attitudes

The quiz you just completed has considerable hidden meaning, which can help you avoid the conformity trap. Each statement in the quiz should be scrutinized to sharpen your insights into conformity. Avoiding the conformity trap, however, does not mean that you avoid all conformity. Instead, find the balance between conformance and independent action. Go along with the team's thinking in most instances, but stay alert to opportunities for independent action.

1. *I rarely question the decision reached by the team.* The stronger your agreement with this question, the stronger your tendencies toward conformity. A key characteristic of the breakthrough team player is the ability and willingness to question and criticize decisions made by the team. Groupthink occurs primarily because no group member is willing to step forward and criticize an outrageous decision by the group. A famous industrial example of groupthink took place at Chrysler Corporation in the 1980s. The management team under Lee Iacocca turned back odometers on automobiles used by Chrysler executives, and sold the cars as brand new. After the deception was discovered, Iacocca admitted the company's guilt and made restitution to the affected customers.

2. *Whatever the group wants is fine with me.* Strong agreement with this question indicates high conformity. Breakthrough team players want to cooperate with the group but establish limits. They will not go along with group desires that clash with their values and independent thinking. At an electronics company in Taiwan, the product development team was ready to sign off on plans to build a copier for PCs strikingly similar in design to the Hewlett-Packard Desk Jet and Laser Jet printers. The name selected for the clone was "Howard Packworth." One of the team members said, "No, we've gone too far in pushing cloning to its legal limits. We've created a knock-off brand that will arouse controversy. We'll be damaging our reputation in the long run just to make some quick sales." The team then decided to manufacture the printer but with a housing and name dissimilar to the Hewlett-Packard models.

3. *My clothing distinguishes me from the other members of the team.* The high-conforming individual disagrees strongly with this statement. He or she succumbs to the pressure of dressing like others and enjoys the uniformity. Although clothing is a superficial aspect of behavior, it is significant. The team player intent on breaking away from the pack is alert to small ways of being distinctive, such as wearing a handkerchief in a jacket pocket or a scarf indoors. Nevertheless, the breakthrough team player establishes a zone for distinctiveness, such as not wearing jeans to a key meeting. Showing up at an office picnic in a dress or business suit also lies outside the zone.

4. *I consider myself to be one of the office gang.* The conformist will usually agree strongly with this statement because he or she finds emotional security in being part of the group. To be labeled "one of the office gang" is a compliment and a source of pride. In contrast, the breakthrough team player has no intention of being indistinguishable from other gang members. He or she wants to be well accepted by the group and perceived as having leadership characteristics. Yet the breakthrough team player attempts to maintain an identity separate from the team.

The person chosen for promotion is usually not somebody who appears to be one of the office gang. In contrast, he or she is a person who appears to identify with higher management.

Despite all the hoopla about team-based organizations and flat-tened organizations, hierarchies still exist. A small, select num-ber of people are chosen for inclusion on top of the pack.

5. *I rarely express disagreement during a group discussion.* The high conformist agrees strongly with this bedrock statement about submission to the group way of thinking. Expressing legit-imate and well-reasoned disagreement is a major strategic tool of the breakthrough team player. As already mentioned, ex-pressing disagreement helps prevent groupthink. Expressing constructive and tactful disagreement also focuses attention on you as an important contributor to the group effort.

To lower the sting of disagreement, express it in positive terms. Suppose the team members are about to agree on a plan that you think is deficient. Instead of disagreeing with the plan, explain that you would agree entirely if certain provisions were added. A plan might be formulated to purchase laptop comput-ers for each team member. In your judgment, however, laptops are often purchased and then used sparingly. You therefore sug-gest that you would support equipping the team with laptops so long as team members are also offered appropriate training.

6. *I routinely have lunch with other members of my team.* High conformers are more likely to routinely have lunch with team members. Lunching with teammates contributes to team spirit and teamwork, and is therefore functional. Yet lunching with teammates exclusively also breeds parochialism that can detract from your freshness of outlook. Lunching with outsiders, or eating by yourself and reading, helps you acquire insights that can enhance your intellectual contribution to the group. Sensi-tivity is required to find the right balance between using lunch as a vehicle for enhancing camaraderie versus networking and information gathering. Becoming a breakthrough team player requires a series of subtle judgments.

7. *My teammates sometimes complain that I think too indepen-dently.* The high conformer rarely suffers from complaints by teammates about independent thinking. He or she succumbs to real or imagined group pressure to avoid independent thinking. In a high-performing organization, the pressure to avoid inde-pendent thinking is mostly imagined. Teams in such organiza-

tions want cooperation combined with independent thinking. Most breakthrough team players would either agree strongly or agree with this statement.

As a breakthrough team player at Chase Corporation put it, "I stand guilty as charged of being a rabble rouser in my thinking." Furthermore, he is on the fast track in the revamped Chase that has overhauled its culture toward better teamwork among units. Thomas G. Labreque, the Chase CEO, wants good teamwork *and* independent thinking. Consistent with the theme of this book, these two goals are not incompatible.

8. *My preference is to piggyback on the ideas of others rather than contribute ideas of my own.* The analysis here is a variation of that presented for the previous question. The high conformist is more likely to take the safe route of piggybacking on the ideas of others than to originate ideas of his own. In this way the conformist can contribute intellectually to the group yet not make waves. In defense of piggybacking, it is a key component of brainstorming. The breakthrough team player may piggyback on the ideas of others, yet will also shift into the role of the person upon whom others piggyback. Original thinking is the hallmark of the breakthrough team player.

9. *When I notice that other members of the team make the same error in speech, I will copy them rather than sound different.* A subtle conforming act is to model the speech patterns of other group members, even when the person might have evidence that the group is wrong. The high conformist is therefore likely to agree strongly or agree with this statement. An effective way of achieving group acceptance is to adapt their speech behaviors. Among such behaviors that are uniformly accepted by the group are jargon and frequently repeated expressions. The breakthrough team player will adapt to many patterns of speech within the group, but will set personal limits. The personal limits often stop at trite or grammatically incorrect expressions.

One popular form of jargon in a bureaucracy is to convert large numbers of nouns into verbs. The bureaucrat will thus sprinkle his or her speech with such phrases as "fax them a message," "photocopy me," "input them," and "overnight this package." To appear distinctive, the breakthrough team player will set limits. For example, the breakthrough player might be willing to use *fax* and *photocopy* as verbs, but not *input* and *overnight*. I brought up this issue with a manager from FedEx (the new official name for Federal Express). She says that her company has absolutely no objection to using "FedEx" as a verb. She would prefer that when you want to send a package overnight, you say "FedEx it."

At the same time, Xerox is opposed to people saying "Xerox this," because people are going to use whatever photocopier the company has, so Xerox gets no financial benefit and could lose trademark status. When you tell someone to "FedEx this," there's a good chance he or she will send it by FedEx instead of using a competitor.

10. *I am often the first person to get up at the scheduled ending time of the meeting.* The high conformer will usually disagree or disagree strongly with being the first to leave a meeting on time. To stay at the meeting until others leave is to submit to group pressure. The more independent thinking team player will take the initiative to leave on schedule. The subtle act of putting your pen or pencil into your pocket or handbag, or picking up your notepad will begin a chain reaction. You will also leave a subliminal message in the minds of others that you are in control at the moment. A breakthrough team player is highly cooperative, yet he or she looks for opportunities to be in control.

11. *I do almost all of my creative thinking for the job when I'm with the team.* A high conformist will tend toward doing most creative thinking in a team setting because he or she wants to work closely with the group. Creative thinking is sometimes enhanced through group problem solving, yet most path-finding ideas are developed by individuals. Solitary reflection is a critical ingredient to the creative process. The creative thinker then brings these ideas into the group for clarification and refinement. Breakthrough team players would tend toward neutral agreement with this issue. They think creatively both when working alone and in groups.

12. *I'm particularly careful not to criticize an idea submitted by a team leader.* Breakthrough team players will criticize ideas submitted by team leaders when appropriate. Yet they are not

attack-people ready to spring at a slight mistake. In a freewheeling, high performance team, members should experience no hesitation in tactfully criticizing the leader's ideas. To be a breakthrough team player, it is necessary to be candid with teammates, including the leader. Diplomacy and statesmanship, however, are still positive leadership characteristics. The high conformist will agree or agree strongly with statements under consideration because he or she does not want to risk rejection by criticizing the leader.

13. *The number of hours I work per week corresponds closely to the number worked by my teammates.* The ultimate conformist adheres strictly to group norms, even to the point of establishing how many hours to work per week and per day. He or she does not want to be perceived as an outcast and therefore ostracized. Most breakthrough team players would take a moderated position on this issue. On the one hand they want to work long and hard enough to accomplish work goals and to advance their careers. On the other hand, breakthrough team players want to maintain cordial relationships with team members. Making it apparent that you work longer and harder than anyone else on the team can put a cordial relationship at risk.

14. *When I think it is necessary, I bring information to the group that conflicts with the path we are following.* Team members with a strong need to conform are often hesitant to bring discordant information to the attention of the group. Bringing forth such information, in their thinking, is an implied criticism of the team effort. The standout team player, in contrast, will bring forth information that conflicts with the path the group is following. He or she does so in a supportive and constructive manner.

Katie is working on an underwriting team in a casualty insurance company. The team is working toward preparing a report that encourages the company to minimize issuing automobile insurance policies for drivers under age twenty-five. Following conventional wisdom, Katie would be supportive of the group's direction. Katie then reads a report that runs counter to conventional wisdom. The combined forces of crashworthy automobiles, a nationwide crackdown on drunk drivers, and more safe-driver education have made insuring young drivers profitable. As a breakthrough team player, Katie brings this information to the team's attention. She says, "I have some vital new information that could alter our recommendations. I wish the team would at least consider these findings before we conclude our report."

15. *I would rather bite my tongue than point out the weaknesses in a teammate's ideas.* A high conformist would agree or agree strongly with this statement. Many people imagine a strong norm exists for not criticizing teammates. Although the breakthrough team player does not relish criticizing teammates, he or she assumes this is an important responsibility. Helping teammates with their thinking in an objective, noninsulting manner contributes to one's leadership stature within the group. Breakthrough team players are therefore likely to disagree or disagree strongly with this statement.

16. *I've been called a maverick on more than one occasion by teammates.* Most high conformists would disagree strongly with the statement that they are regarded as mavericks by teammates. A high conformer would shudder at the thought of thinking too independently. Most breakthrough team players are not total mavericks because they work within the structure of a team. Yet their thinking is radical enough on occasion that they would typically respond "agree" to this statement. A maverick is likely to be creative, which is an asset for a breakthrough team player.

17. *I encourage team members to express doubts about proposed solutions to problems.* Encouraging doubts about proposed solutions to problems is a high-level skill of the breakthrough team player. The high conformist is unlikely to engage in this behavior because it encourages disharmony within the group. He or she would therefore be likely to disagree or disagree strongly with this statement. The breakthrough team player looks for disagreement that can improve decision making, but does not relentlessly pursue disagreement. Developing the reputation of one who encourages constructive controversy can help the person achieve individual recognition within the group. A member

of a process redesign team within a Prudential unit describes his behavior toward encouraging doubt and criticism:

> Whether or not I'm given the title of team leader, I think it's important to provoke pointed discussion. If we don't get disagreements out on the table, we're not taking advantage of the full power of the group.

18. *I invite criticism of my ideas.* This statement has an indirect and subtle relationship to conformity. High conformers do not welcome criticism of their ideas because criticism points to areas where their thinking deviates from the group norm. High conformers will also disagree or disagree strongly with this statement because it breeds conflict and disagreement. The breakthrough team player would most likely agree strongly or agree with the statement, "I invite criticism of my ideas." He or she reasons that criticism leads to refinement of thinking, which in turn leads to higher-quality solutions to problems. In turn, high-quality solutions to problems lead to better contributions and more recognition even if the link is not direct.

19. *When the team laughs at a comment, I laugh too, even if I don't think the comment was funny.* Laughing at comments that are intended to be funny is an effective political tactic. The insecure high conformer will consistently laugh at comments others think are funny, even if he or she does not get the point of the humor. To do otherwise is to deviate from group behavior, thus risking rejection. A breakthrough team player is typically neutral on this issue. To be an outstanding team player one must be a first-rate office politician, but not an absolute sycophant. Mr. or Ms. Breakthrough might not break out in laughter in response to a comment he or she did not think was funny. Nevertheless, he or she might at least smile warmly so as not to reject the person who made the comment.

20. *Most of my social life centers around activities with my teammates.* High-conforming team players struggle so hard for group acceptance that they prefer to center most of their social life around teammates. High conformers would therefore agree strongly or agree with this statement. Part of the high conformer's reason for focusing social life on teammates is that he or she thinks it is expected behavior.

The breakthrough team player is most likely to disagree or disagree strongly with the idea of centering social life around teammates. He or she wants cordial relationships with the group but still maintains a modicum of psychological distance from team members. The distance helps the breakthrough team player step away from the group when a broader assignment presents itself. Breakthrough team players, however, regularly attend company-sponsored social functions. To do otherwise is to project disinterest in the team and the larger organization.

Geography is a key influence on the extent to which teammates spend much time together socially. In large metropolitan areas, workmates typically scatter in many directions after work, some workers living as much as seventy-five miles apart from each other. In smaller towns, workmates live closer to each other. In addition, people working together in small towns feel a greater kinship toward each other.

How Status Within the Team Affects Conformity

A key fact about conformity not implied in the quiz deserves separate mention. Conformity to group norms is much more pronounced among low-status than high-status individuals. Low-status members of the group (such as a newcomer with an unknown reputation) are usually concerned about how much influence they possess. Low-status members will therefore tread lightly when being critical of the team's accepted beliefs and values. The following case history illustrates this point.

Pam, a manufacturing engineer, was invited to join a product development team whose mission was to design a new clothes washer and dryer. During the first several meetings, established members of the team said that the new design should build on the strengths of the existing machine. As the group perceived the situation, a key strength was the exquisite control panels on the washers and driers. Pam, however, thought that the complex panels were a design flaw. Her perception was that the vast majority of owners used only two or three settings. The complex control panel was therefore fluff that increased costs and created greater exposure to malfunctioning.

Instead of being forthright in her criticism, Pam only hinted at her concern about building a control panel that was contributing little to customer satisfaction. The revised machines were built with more elaborate control panels than the existing models. The new generation of washers and dryers sold less well than the previous ones. Pam felt guilty for not having expressed her individual opinion.

If Pam had had more status within the group, she might have had the confidence to make her reservations explicit. The message here is to be on guard not to let your status within the group hold you back from candor. Without tactfully criticizing what needs to be criticized, you will not become a breakthrough team player.

Retaining Your Individuality

A major philosophical and career-survival issue in a team-based workplace is how to retain your individuality. The philosophical issue is that many people want to retain their individual identity in spite of being a member of a larger organization. By retaining your individuality you resist conforming too tightly to group norms. The career-survival issue is that by preserving your individuality, you can attain the recognition needed for career advancement. I am not suggesting that you surrender your status as an outstanding team player. The trick is to retain your individuality *and* be a high-performing team player.

Several ways to avoid being a conformist—thus preserving your individuality—have been suggested in the analysis of The Conformity Quiz. For example, you might wear distinctive clothing, express independent thoughts, and not center your social life around teammates. Here are additional strategies and tactics for retaining your individuality while still being a good team member.

1. *Be distinctive in some meaningful way.* Act and speak slightly differently from the way others in the group do. If they take notes with an inexpensive plastic ballpoint pen, you take notes with a luxury pen or laptop computer. If other team members stay seated to make a point, you stand up on occasion. Point to the flip chart with a laser spotlight (they resemble a fountain-pen size flashlight) if others simply wave their arms.

2. *Be willing to say "The emperor has no clothes" if it is true.* A loyal team member avoids routinely challenging the actions and thoughts of higher management. However, at times it pays to constructively criticize the direction in which the company or the organization is headed.

An accountant won praise from higher management because she said during a team meeting that she was concerned about the company's recent divestitures. (The CEO was divesting so the company could return to its core businesses.) Her reasoning was that the company needed the hedge that diversification could provide. Her statement helped convince top management to not sell one of the business units earmarked for divestment. When the accountant first made her statement, several other members of the team said she should not openly criticize company strategy.

3. *Initiate action rather than waiting for someone else to change your environment.* An outstanding characteristic of a high-achieving individual is the willingness and capability to initiate action.[2] One activity a team cannot do well is to initiate ideas. Team members may build on an idea generated by one person, but all the team members are not likely to have the same thought at once. Suppose, for example, you believe the team is spending far too much time on trivial issues. Rather than grumble about all the time in your work week devoted to team interaction, state your case. Take the initiative to say that you think the team would be more productive if it met less frequently, and spent less time on trivial issues.

2. Ibid., p. 128.

4. *Depart occasionally from the conventional mode of doing things.* Search for opportunities to engage in unconventional modes of doing things that are still beneficial to the team and organization. Ask for permission to spend one half-day per week working at home. Explain that you need the quiet time for planning. Ask the group for permission to bring in an outsider from another type of organization to give the team a fresh perspective. If your team is performing high-level work, conduct interviews with entry-level workers to obtain their input on the topic.

5. *Initiate a discussion with a confidante as to whether that person thinks you have crossed the line between being a good team player and being a 1990s version of the "organization person."* The "organization man" of the 1950s was a high-conforming person who maintained job security by avoiding controversy and being a yes-man. If you have become an organization person in the eyes of other people, you are probably falling short of being a breakthrough team player.

6. *Become a renegade team member for the good of the organization.* A renegade thinker, in this context, is one who challenges the team to depart radically from the usual way of doing business. You express your individuality by encouraging the group to take a giant leap forward, in much the way an entrepreneur would start a dramatically new business. Similarly, you might act like an intrapreneur. An *intrapreneur* is a corporate employee who is funded by the organization to start a dramatic new venture.

Several years back a member of the customer-service team at the Milford Plaza Hotel in New York City was concerned that customer-service improvements at the hotel were too minor. The renegade team member proposed that the hotel radically reduce the amount of time required for checking out. She located a vendor who developed a checkout machine that enabled guests to check themselves out by inserting a credit card into the machine. Still in operation, the machine became a prototype for automatic hotel checkouts. The team member in question distinguished herself and is now an executive in the parent company of the hotel.

A Team Structure to Encourage Individual Initiative

A key weakness of many teams is that they stifle creativity and initiative. While sitting in meetings, members are sometimes lulled into thinking alike and not wanting to make waves. The solutions proposed for problems are often vanilla flavored when an exotic new flavor is required. Not all teams fall prey to this conformity trap, but stifling of initiative and creativity can be a problem.

When the organization needs visionary new initiatives, such as entering a new market or redesigning major business processes, it is best to use a team structure that enhances high-level creativity and initiative. Stanley H. Herman has proposed a team structure, the *individual initiative network*, designed for such a purpose.[3] It is a team composed of high-performing volunteers who contribute to and support each other's initiatives. Much like a task force, people may work on the team part-time, as needed. Working within such a structure should facilitate a person in becoming a breakthrough team player.

The individual initiative network is usually set up to respond to a current problem or to pursue an opportunity. In one insurance company, two information technology experts collaborated with the vice president of administration to explore the feasibility of reengineering the sales, claims, and underwriting divisions. After studying these business processes for two months, the company decided to embark on a reengineering program.

Reengineering consultants were hired, who worked with the members of the individual initiative network. Also, a small task force was formed to work with the consultants. Most of the work performed in the major departments was given over to business process teams. Customer service improved because

3. Ibid., p. 165–169.

policies were now issued more promptly. Of greater importance to customers, claims were now settled more quickly.

The initiative network is a special type of task force, small in size, and driven by an unambiguous purpose. The team is expected to work intensely for a short period of time and achieve its goal. Team members are driven by a purpose and are expected to sell that purpose to others. A highly focused, visible task force of this type is ideal for the breakthrough team player because of the high-recognition value of membership. Similar to intrapreneurs, members of an individual initiative network are willing to risk company money and their reputation for their cause.

Members of these teams have little concern about conformity, often resembling the inventive, egocentric, and driven entrepreneur. Irreverent thinking among them is not uncommon. One member of the insurance company network commented frequently, "I don't care how long the department has been doing it this way. It doesn't mean it's right." Despite their cantankerousness, network members conform enough to contribute mightily to a high-performance team. Much like other breakthrough team players, outstanding performance is their goal. At the same time they enjoy working collaboratively with others.

Assuming that you have found the right balance between conforming to group expectations and still retaining uniqueness of thought and actions, you are now prepared to face another key activity for the breakthrough team player: selecting one or more roles on the team.

4

Choosing Team Player Roles

To the casual observer a team meeting appears to be a group of people seated around a table talking, arguing, joking, smiling, frowning, yawning, taking notes, drinking coffee and soft drinks, and getting up for breaks. All of these observations are correct. On the surface, team meetings do not appear different from any gathering of businesspeople. Yet the external and superficial aspects of behavior don't show a critical process that takes place within a team both during and outside of meetings.

During the life of a team, various members occupy different roles, or sets of behaviors, that contribute mightily to the success or failure of the team. Furthermore, the same person may carry out various roles depending on the individual's inclinations and the needs of the moment. Recognizing and understanding these roles can help you become a bigger contributor to the team's effort. Your enlarged contribution will in turn help you to become a breakthrough team player. In addition to understanding the various roles, an effective team player stays alert to the need for occupying different roles at various times.

The information in this chapter is organized into three sections: grabbing the leadership reins by becoming an informal leader within the team; team-enhancing roles, and team-subverting roles. But before reading further, take the accompanying self-quiz. It will get you started thinking about the roles you may have played or will be playing as a team member.

The Team Player Quiz

Directions: Check either "mostly agree" or "mostly disagree" for each of the following statements about team activity. If you have not experienced a situation, imagine how you would act or think if you were placed in that situation. Fill out the questionnaire with the intention of learning something about yourself.

	Mostly Agree	Mostly Disagree
1. It is rare that I ever miss a team meeting.	_____	_____
2. I regularly compliment team members when they do something exceptional.	_____	_____
3. Whenever I can, I avoid being the note-taker at a team meeting.	_____	_____
4. From time to time, other team members come to me for advice on technical matters.	_____	_____
5. I like to hide some information from other team members so I can be in control.	_____	_____
6. I welcome new team members' coming to me for advice and learning the ropes.	_____	_____
7. My priorities come first, which leaves me with very little time to help other team members.	_____	_____
8. During a team meeting, it is not unusual for several other people at a time to look toward me for my opinion.	_____	_____
9. If I think the team is moving in an unethical direction, I will say so explicitly.	_____	_____
10. Rarely will I criticize the progress of the team even if I think such criticism is deserved.	_____	_____
11. It's not unusual for me to summarize the progress in a team meeting, even if I am not asked.	_____	_____
12. To conserve time, I attempt to minimize contact with my teammates outside of our meetings.	_____	_____
13. I intensely dislike going along with a consensus decision if the decision runs contrary to my thoughts on the issue.	_____	_____

		Mostly Agree	Mostly Disagree
14.	I rarely remind teammates of our mission statement as we go about our work.	————	————
15.	Once I have made up my mind on an issue facing the team, I am unlikely to be persuaded in another direction.	————	————
16.	I am willing to accept negative feedback from team members.	————	————
17.	Just to get a new member of the team involved, I will ask his or her opinion.	————	————
18.	Even if the team has decided on a course of action, I am not hesitant to bring in new information that supports another position.	————	————
19.	Quite often I talk negatively about one team member to another.	————	————
20.	My teammates are almost a family to me, because I am truly concerned about their welfare.	————	————
21.	When it seems appropriate, I joke and kid with teammates.	————	————
22.	My contribution to team tasks is as important to me as my individual work.	————	————
23.	From time to time I have pointed out to the team how we can all improve in reaching our goals.	————	————
24.	I will fight to the end when the team does not support my viewpoint and wants to move toward consensus.	————	————
25.	I will confront the team if I believe that the members are thinking too much alike.	————	————

Total Score ————

Scoring and interpretation: Give yourself a plus one for each statement you gave that matches the key that follows. The keyed answer indicates a carrying out of a positive role.

Question Number	Positive Role Answer	Question Number	Positive Role Answer
1.	Mostly Agree	14.	Mostly Disagree
2.	Mostly Agree	15.	Mostly Disagree
3.	Mostly Disagree	16.	Mostly Agree
4.	Mostly Agree	17.	Mostly Agree
5.	Mostly Disagree	18.	Mostly Agree
6.	Mostly Agree	19.	Mostly Disagree
7.	Mostly Disagree	20.	Mostly Agree
8.	Mostly Agree	21.	Mostly Agree
9.	Mostly Agree	22.	Mostly Agree
10.	Mostly Disagree	23.	Mostly Agree
11.	Mostly Disagree	24.	Mostly Disagree
12.	Mostly Disagree	25.	Mostly Agree
13.	Mostly Disagree		

20–25   You carry out a well-above-average number of positive team roles. Behavior of this type contributes substantially to being a breakthrough team player. Study the information in this chapter to build upon your already laudable sensitivity to occupying various positive roles within the team.

10–19   You carry out an average number of positive team roles. Study carefully the roles described in this chapter to search for ways to carry out a greater number of positive roles. You will need this increase in positive roles to become a breakthrough team player.

0–9   You carry out a substantially above-average number of negative team roles. If becoming a breakthrough team player is important to you, you will have to assiduously search for ways to play positive team roles. Study the information in this chapter carefully.

Grabbing the Leadership Reins

When a team is formed by the organization, the typical procedure is to appoint a leader or manager. Following this procedure, Kathy is appointed project manager, Gerry is named the committee head, and Sherri is given the title of chair of the task force. Kathy, Gerry, and Sherri are classified as *formal leaders* because the organization has granted them authority to be responsible for managing their groups.

In an ultrademocratic organization, a group may be formed (such as a self-governing work team) in which the team is granted the authority to appoint a leader. The team then reaches consensus on which member is granted the title of team leader. The team leader is also classified as a formal leader because he or she was formally appointed by organizational representatives.

The person designated as a formal leader exercises position power, because he or she occupies a position that carries the right to engage in certain actions. Among these actions are conducting performance appraisals, making recommendations for salary adjustments, promotion, and termination. An effective formal leader, however, exercises power in other ways referred to as personal power. The leader can be charming and emotionally expressive. As a consequence, he or she exercises power through being charismatic. The person can also exercise power through possessing technical expertise and other key information needed by the team. (As presented in detail below, you don't have to be the formal leader to exercise personal power.)

If this time around you are not appointed as the formal leader, there is still opportunity for you to practice *informal leadership*. You can carry out both overt and subtle leadership roles without benefiting from the formal title of leader. Breakthrough team players seize the opportunity to grab the leadership reins for two important reasons. First, they want to maximize their contribution to the group. Taking on leadership responsibility enlarges one's contribution to the group. Second, breakthrough team players have an eye on the future. They know that team players who are perceived as exercising leadership within the team are strong candidates for formal leadership responsibility.

Here I will describe the two sources of power the team member has that enable him or her to exercise informal leadership: expert power and referent power. Accompanying each source of power will be examples of how it can be exercised by a team member. The general approach is to be aware of the two sources of power, and then be alert to opportunities to exercise that power. To do otherwise is to fall short of becoming a breakthrough team player.

Expert Power

Expert power is the ability to influence others through specialized knowledge skills or abilities. If you are the expert for the team on a topic of importance to the team's mission, you can exercise expert power. Two examples:

[SCENARIO 1]

The team is poring over results of a survey. One of the findings is that 85 percent of customers rated service as "very good or excellent" this quarter. For the same quarter last year, 81 percent of customers responded in the same way.

Team members seem pleased. All eyes turn toward you as you say, "I want to be pleased as much as you do. But before we can be sure our customer satisfaction ratings have increased a reliable amount, we must run some probability statistics. I can find out this afternoon if there is a statistically significant difference between then and now."

[*Your esoteric knowledge of statistics will prevent the team arriving at a naive conclusion. Because other members of the team lack statistical knowledge, you have exercised leadership in this issue. Score one for being a breakthrough team player.*]

[SCENARIO 2]

Your team is developing an advertising campaign targeted to the Hispanic market. The campaign will appear in Spanish-language newspapers, magazines, and television. The centerpiece of the ad is an attractive young woman walking down the street alone wearing your company's brand of clothing. The team is excited about the ad because it is so refreshing and uplifting. Other team members turn to you intently as you say, "I'm excited about this ad also, because it is so uplifting. However, my knowledge of the Hispanic culture tells me that we are repeating a mistake that a jeans manufacturer tried before."

The Hispanic culture emphasizes gregariousness. The preferred image is people walking down the street accompanied by friends, holding hands at times, smiling, and laughing. Hispanics would not be impressed by a woman walking down the street alone. "Have that lovely woman walk down the street with two or three other people," you say, "and we've got a winner."

[*Score one for using your cross-cultural sensitivity to help your team emerge victorious and not repeat a blooper made previously by a jeans manufacturer.*]

Referent Power

The ability to control others based on loyalty to the leader and the team members' desire to please that person is referent power. Charisma is the basis of referent power. We ordinarily think of formal leaders as having charisma, yet other team members can be charismatic. The following aspects of charisma can be achieved by a team member as well as a leader:

1. *Provide vision.* Extremely charismatic leaders offer a vision of where the organization is headed and how to get there. You can sometimes do the same for your team even acting as an informal leader. A vision is more than a forecast, because it describes an ideal version of the future.

2. *Communicate masterfully.* Charismatic leaders spin believable dreams and portray their vision of the future as the only way to go. They use metaphors to inspire people, such as "I know our company has been through bankruptcy. But believe me, we are like the phoenix. We will arise from the ashes and fly overhead victoriously. Join me in this beautiful and peaceful flight that is ours for the taking."

3. *Inspire trust.* Charismatic leaders inspire such confidence in team members that the members are willing to risk their careers to pursue their leader's vision. To strengthen the perception that they are effective leaders, they take the initiative to get recognition for their accomplishments. They toot their own horn without being embarrassed. You too can make your accomplishments known to your teammates, so you will inspire trust in your leadership capabilities.

4. *Help group members feel capable.* Charismatic leaders help group members feel capable. You can help your teammates feel capable by instructing them in skills you possess but they do not. Janet, a member of a cost-reduction team, showed two teammates the rudiments of WordPerfect 6.0 (a comprehensive word-processing package). Both people became more confident of their computer skills and were therefore indebted to Janet.

5. *Express positive emotions openly.* Expressing feelings openly is an especially important way of being charismatic. Freely express warmth, joy, happiness, and enthusiasm in your interactions with teammates. It will contribute to your informal leadership status.[1]

[SCENARIO 1]

You belong to a mergers and acquisitions team. You have been working for a year on acquiring another company that would complement your firm's product line and open new channels of distribution. As negotiations run down to the wire, you and your teammates have been working 70 hours per week. The team leader calls the group together to present the outcome of your hard work. He informs you that an investment group offered more for the target company than your firm did. The board of directors of the company in question has voted to be purchased by the investment company. A pall hits the team.

You look at your teammates and say, "We're all hard

1. Jay A. Conger, *The Charismatic Leader: Beyond the Mystiques of Exceptional Leadership* (San Francisco: Jossey-Bass, 1989).

hit by this unfortunate turn of events. We have lost out on this big deal even after working so hard. But I'm proud of the proposal we put together. It shows how knowledgeable we have become in the mergers-and-acquisition game. I bet we acquire the next company we try to snag." You then smile warmly at your teammates.

[*Your comments are well timed, and you have shown elements of charisma. You have communicated well, you have made your teammates feel capable, and you smiled warmly at a time when it was needed.*]

[Scenario 2]

You are part of a process-improvement team whose purpose is to simplify and clarify orders from dealers. During the third meeting of your team, the process manager (a.k.a. the team leader) suggests that a subteam be formed to investigate how dealers perceive your company's order process. Instead of staring down at the table to avoid being appointed to this subteam, you seize the initiative. You say to the process manager and your other teammates, "Here's a wonderful opportunity to get the information we need to do an outstanding job. Besides, we should get to know our dealers—the people who pay our salaries."

[*Your energy, excitement, and enthusiasm are shining through. You will be remembered as a charismatic contributor to process improvement. Don't worry about somebody accusing you of kissing up to the process manager. It's the enthusiasts who get the most organizational rewards, and therefore become breakthrough team players.*]

In summary: to become an informal leader, encourage your teammates to gravitate toward you. Ordinarily you can achieve this through expert power, referent power, or a combination of the two. Find a way to distinguish yourself through your knowledge, your physical and psychological presence, or both. Learn a task-relevant skill the other members don't have, and be willing to share your expertise.

Team-Enhancing Roles

A useful way of understanding roles carried out by team players is to classify roles as positive or negative. The positive roles enhance team effectiveness. In contrast, negative roles subvert the major purposes of the team. My thinking about positive and negative roles has been influenced by the research, writing, and consulting experiences of Glenn M. Parker and Thomas L. Quick. The remaining two sections of this chapter are based heavily on their analyses.[2] My firsthand observations of teams strongly support the conclusions drawn by Parker and Quick. We begin with an analysis of the team-enhancing roles so characteristic of breakthrough team players.

Knowledge Contributor

A technically knowledgeable team member, the Knowledge Contributor provides the group with useful and valid information. He or she is a facts and figures person who is intent upon helping the team with task accomplishment. The Knowledge Contributor believes it is important to share technical expertise with team members. He or she does consider the human element in a team setting, but does so primarily in order to help get the task accomplished. A financial specialist on a cross-functional team explains how the human factor can enter into work dealing with facts and figures:

> As the financial expert on the team, I had to explain the reasoning behind a sales forecast I developed. To really understand this forecast, a person had to know basic calculus. Unfortunately the person I was explaining the forecast to had zero knowledge of calculus. I

2. Glenn M. Parker, *Team Players and Teamwork: The New Competitive Business Strategy* (San Francisco: Jossey-Bass, 1990), pp. 61–98; Thomas L. Quick, *Successful Team Building* (New York: AMACOM, 1992), pp. 40–52.

had to calm down his anxieties enough so he could listen to me. I explained several times that very few people in customer service understood calculus. He then stopped being so defensive, and I could get on with showing the validity of my forecast.

As the financial expert's experience illustrates, a major behavior of the Knowledge Contributor is to share knowledge freely with teammates. Rarely will they hoard knowledge to maintain an edge over others in the group. Knowledge sharing is important for training others and contributes to the Knowledge Contributor's potential for being a breakthrough team player. At times the Knowledge Contributor will spend so much time helping others that he or she has to work extra hours to complete individual assignments.

Knowledge Contributors take considerable pride in the written reports and oral presentations they make to the group. In their thinking, all the work they produce is a self-portrait; it reflects on their character. If they are assigned to a team part-time (as are most team assignments), they still find time to accomplish all their assigned work in their functional departments.

In short, the Knowledge Contributor is the hard-working technical expert on the team who performs reliably. He or she gladly trains teammates, and sometimes serves as a mentor. Breakthrough team players all spend at least part of their time occupying the Knowledge Contributor role.

Process Observer

Dealing with knowledge, technology, and methodology are indispensable for group achievement—the *hard* side of collective effort. Another key aspect of a team's work is the processes that take place within the group. This *soft* side of teamwork includes the transactions that take place between members of the team. Among the dozens of processes within a team are political infighting, soothing feelings, forming coalitions, communicating problems, complimenting each other, and complementing one another. Add to this list careful listening, interrupting each other, expressing anger, and relieving tension. If you reflect back on your experiences in group assignments, you can probably pinpoint numerous processes that you witnessed.

The Process Observer forces the group to look at how it is functioning, with statements such as: "Look, gang. We've been at it for two-and-one-half hours, and we have only taken care of one agenda item. Shouldn't we be doing better?" On the positive side, the Process Observer might point to any excellent progress that the team has made. The Process Observer spends only a small amount of time observing how the group is functioning, but these observations can be instrumental in the accomplishment of the group's tasks. A breakthrough team player should therefore devote some time to process observation.

Process observation is recognized by specialists in the field as essential for successful group functioning. Some companies hire outside process consultants to attend team meetings occasionally to analyze group processes. In the group problem-solving model widely used at Xerox Corporation, each team assigns one member to carry out the role of Process Observer. One person who took over this role for several meetings said, "I felt like a pest at first. Yet I soon realized that I was making a real contribution to the success of our team."

Collaborator

Another key team player role is the person who pitches in to do whatever is necessary to achieve team goals and is not constrained by his or her official responsibilities. The Collaborator keeps the team focused on its goal and frequently reminds the group to do whatever is necessary to stay on track. A Collaborator's typical behavior during a team meeting would be to indicate how much progress the team has made toward goal attainment. A representative comment would be, "We are halfway through our time budget, and we have achieved one-fourth of our goals. We are behind schedule, but catching up is doable."

As a football player, a Collaborator would play offense and defense, and drive the bus if the assigned driver became ill during a trip. As the manager of a supermarket, the Collaborator would open up another lane and work as a cashier if lines were backing up. The Collaborator works for the good of the group and does not care who gets recognition as long as the job gets done. Being so self-sacrificing, the Collaborator may fall short of becoming a breakthrough team player. He or she often works quietly behind the scenes and does not look for individual recognition.

People Supporter

A well-accepted leadership practice is for the leader to support group members, thus facilitating communication, reducing tension, and elevating morale. The People Supporter on the team assumes some of the responsibility for providing emotional support to teammates and resolving conflict. He or she serves as a model of active listening when others are presenting. The People Supporter helps others relax by smiling, making humorous comments, and appearing relaxed. However, he or she should not be confused with the team clown, who attempts to defuse the seriousness of a situation, but in contrast is a model of etiquette and professionalism.

The People Supporter reinforces the views of other team members with which he or she agrees. Most team players find this to be a comfortable role. What distinguishes People Supporters is their additional willingness to support and encourage team members with whom they disagree. The People Supporter believes that anybody who is serious about his or her position on an issue deserves encouragement. By receiving encouragement now, the person is more likely to contribute ideas in the future.

Mary is a member of a quality-improvement team at a county clerk's office in New Jersey. Her actions on the team indicate her dominant role as People Supporter. Mary was asked why she is constantly so supportive and friendly as a team member. She responded:

First of all, I'm supportive by nature. I've always been that way on the job and at home. Now that I'm part of the quality revolution, being supportive is more important than ever. The suggestions made by a quality-improvement team are only as good as the ideas contributed by individual members. You get the most from people if you show respect for their ideas. Putdowns lead to shutdowns in communication.

I used to work for a boss who believed that dissension in the group kept people from getting too lethargic. He would therefore antagonize people just to keep them alert. I disagree entirely with his philosophy. You get better ideas for quality improvement when people do not feel threatened and are relaxed.

Being a People Supporter contributes substantially to becoming a breakthrough team player. As a People Supporter, you become recognized for your calming influence on the team. The ability to resolve conflict in such a way that high-quality decisions are reached is a notable contribution.

Challenger

To prevent complacency and groupthink, a team needs one or more members who will confront and challenge ideas that should be confronted and challenged. The Challenger fills this role, if he or she has effective enough interpersonal skills. Antagonistic, attack-style people who attempt the Challenger role lose their credibility quickly. A Challenger will criticize any decision or preliminary thinking of the team that is deficient in any way, including being ethically unsound. An accomplished Challenger will even criticize the methods and decision-making process of a team.

The Challenger role is more specific and focused than most of the roles described in this chapter. A list of Challenger behaviors is therefore warranted:

1. Candidly expresses views about the output of the team
2. Disagrees openly with team leadership when he or she believes disagreement is warranted
3. Questions the relevancy of the team's mission and goals
4. Prods the team to establish high ethical standards

5. Expresses own opinion even when that view is in opposition to the majority of the team's opinion
6. Asks provocative questions, such as "Why?" "How?" "With whose money?" "When?" and "For what purpose?"
7. Encourages the team to take sensible risks
8. Honestly analyzes team progress and problems facing the team
9. Blows the whistle on illegal and unethical activities of the team
10. Backs off when views are not accepted and supports a legitimate team consensus [Although the Challenger slips into the role of being a detached critic, he or she still remains a good team player.][3]

Because Challengers are such provocateurs and deviate from conventional wisdom, they are sometimes accused of being poor team players. However, the Challenger is one step ahead of the pack and may well become a breakthrough team player. He or she knows that challenging the status quo is one of many requirements of the independent thinker and leader.

Here is a transcript of a small portion of a team meeting in which Ruth is the Challenger.

Carlos is the team leader. The team was formed within a service organization. The purpose of forming the team was to develop suggestions for reducing costs throughout the organization.

Carlos: We've been gathering information for a month now. It's about time we heard some of the specific suggestions.
Jack: At the top of my list is cutting pension benefits. Our pension payments are higher than those required by law. Our medical benefits are way above average. If we cut back on pension benefits, no current employees would be adversely affected.

---

3. List adapted from Parker, *Team Players and Teamwork*, p. 85.

Melissa: I like your analysis, Jack. No sense risking laying off employees just to keep retirees happy.

Jordan: We should first make absolutely certain there are no legal complications here. Then we can sharpen our cost-cutting knives and dig right in.

Gunther: I'd support cutting pension benefits. It would probably reduce expenses more dramatically than the ways that I have uncovered.

Carlos: There seems to be consensus so far that we should consider making recommendations about cutting pension benefits? Ruth, what do you think?

Ruth: I think it is much too early to reach consensus on such a sensitive issue. Cutting pension benefits would create panic in our retirees. Our older employees would be screaming as well. We'll have an avalanche of negative publicity in the media.

Jordan: Hold on, Ruth. I said the team should first check out this idea with the legal department.

Ruth: Just because cutting pension benefits could squeeze by legally doesn't mean it's a good idea. We haven't examined the negative ramifications of cutting pension benefits. Let's study this issue further before word leaks out that we're taking away the golden egg.

Carlos: Maybe Ruth has a point. Let's investigate this issue further before making a recommendation.

Listener

Listening to others is an important aspect of several team player roles, including the Supporter. Nevertheless, listening contributes so substantially to team success that it constitutes a separate role. If people are not heard, the full contribution of team effort cannot be realized. Listening takes hard work and commitment, with the Listener serving as a model for the rest of the group.

Some people neglect slipping into the Listener role when appropriate or required, because they are so preoccupied with their own points of view and agendas. Think back to recent meetings you have attended. Do you remember some people starting their counterargument before the speaker has finished his or her sentence? Another reason some team members do not listen is that they become close-minded and defensive when their views are challenged.

The team leader must shift frequently into the Listener role, as Carlos did when he listened carefully to Ruth's concerns about cutting the pension benefits. Other members of the team also must seize the opportunity to occupy the Listener role. This person listens intently to elicit information, understand the opinion or data being presented, and increase the satisfaction of another member. The breakthrough team player devotes ample time to occupying a Listener role. Most readers are familiar with the basics of listening. Here is a sampling of advanced listening behaviors for team members:

- Look intently at the person who is speaking, and at the same time nod your head in approval periodically.
- Move your chair toward the speaker.
- When the person talking pauses, you murmur, "This is good. This is really good."
- Concentrate intently on the presenter, searching for the emotion behind the facts. Assume that a team member says, "We seem to be about on schedule," in a tentative voice. Searching for the feelings behind the facts, you might ask, "What do you mean exactly by *about* on schedule?"

Summarizer

So many details and varied points arise during team meetings that confusion may result. Members may ask themselves "Where are we?" or "What's going on here?" At other times, several group members may forget the purpose of the meeting.

The Summarizer will step in to summarize and clarify, thus giving the team time to pause and reflect. A brief and accurate summary clarifies some of the uncertainty. As Thomas L. Quick reports, a summary also helps because it may restore the team's confidence by showing that the team has made more progress than anybody thought. In addition, a summary can point the way toward unfinished tasks.[4] During a team meeting about improving customer satisfaction, a person carrying out the Summarizer role presented the following summary:

> I know several of you have been frustrated with what
> we have accomplished so far. I think we deserve more
> credit than we have given ourselves. After several
> meetings, we have identified eleven aspects of our ser-
> vice disliked by customers. We do not have solutions
> yet, but we at least have identified the main problem
> areas. We now know what has to be done next.

Presenting summaries to the group contributes to your status as a breakthrough team player. People who can synthesize and clarify are perceived as exercising leadership. And breakthrough team players at their best are leaders.

Conciliator

Strong disagreements often arise in an emotion-packed team meeting. Two people may be engaged in a debate and focus so much on areas of disagreement that they ignore their areas of agreement. Subgroups within the team may experience the same misperception. A related problem is that in the passion of team activity, members may forget their *superordinate purpose* (the grand purpose or mission toward which they are all working).

Enter the Conciliator, who helps opposing sides find areas of agreement and remember their superordinate purpose. At the headquarters of a multinational company, a team was appointed to design a training and development program for company personnel being given assignments abroad. Two of the team members heatedly debated the best content for the program. One insisted the program should concentrate on international business topics, such as trade and tariff regulations and currency exchange rates. The other team member insisted the most important developmental need was for expatriates to understand the culture, customs, and language of the host country. The two

4. Quick, *Successful Team Building*, p. 42.

combatants would occasionally drop their argument, only to re-introduce the topic shortly thereafter.

The Conciliator in the group finally raised her hand and presented this analysis: "Both of you are making valid points, but you are being too parochial. The one area of agreement I hear is that you both want our expatriates to be well prepared for their overseas assignments. Maybe our development program should contain an even mixture of international business and cultural relations."

Mediator

The term *team* implies that people are working together to achieve a collective purpose. Despite good intentions, disputes within the group may become so intense or prolonged that two people no longer listen or respond to each other. The two antagonists develop such polarized viewpoints that they are unwilling to compromise. They have moved beyond the point where conciliation is effective. Instead, it becomes necessary for the team leader or a team member to mediate the dispute. The Mediator attempts to resolve the conflict, following these steps:

1. Asks permission to interpret each position
2. Interprets each side, and then asks both parties if the interpretation is accurate
3. Gives each side the opportunity to edit or correct the statement of his or her position

The Mediator's intervention helps clarify for both sides what each has said. In the heat of the dispute, each side may not have listened carefully to the other. After the three-step intervention is completed, other members of the team can discuss the differences in viewpoint. Mediation makes a contribution because it moves a group away from being stuck and on to more productive activity.

Gatekeeper

A recurring problem in group efforts is that some members may fail to contribute because most of the time has been hogged by dominant team members. Even when the viewpoints of the timid team members have been expressed, they may not be remembered because one or two other members contribute so frequently to discussion. When the opportunity gate is closed to several members, the Gatekeeper in the group intentionally opens it. The Gatekeeper requests that a specific team member be allowed to contribute, or that his or her past contribution be recognized. Here is a sampling of Gatekeeper requests:

> "Alice has been trying for fifteen minutes to make a point. We've all been talking so much that she hasn't found room to talk. I think it's Alice's turn."

> "I've heard several times that Pam's idea enabled us to move in a new direction. I agree that Pam has given us a lot of useful ideas. However, the idea that put us in a new direction was first contributed by Salvatore last week. Let's give him proper credit."

> "Tom, you've been using much more than your share of our discussion time. Since this is a team effort, we need to hear from other people on the team also."

Breakthrough team players are eager to slip into the Gatekeeper role because it gives them the opportunity to help others and demonstrate their interpersonal skills at the same time.

The many positive roles just presented overlap somewhat. For example, the Process Observer might engage in Gatekeeper activities. Do not be concerned about the overlap. Instead, pick and choose from the many roles as the situation dictates whether or not overlap exists. The accompanying list summarizes the various positive roles.

Positive Team Player Roles

- Knowledge Contributor
- Process Observer
- Collaborator
- People Supporter
- Challenger
- Listener
- Summarizer
- Conciliator
- Mediator
- Gatekeeper

Team-Subverting Roles

In an effort be an effective team player, some people may inadvertently carry out roles that subvert rather than enhance team effectiveness. Any one of the team-enhancing roles described earlier could backfire if carried to excess. The Summarizer, for example, might consume too much time belaboring the obvious. And a Challenger who played the role too conscientiously might become an antagonistic force within the team. Brief descriptions are presented in this section of team-subverting roles. You can use this information to alert you to actions that could lower team productivity and morale. The same actions could prevent you from becoming a breakthrough team player.

Ineffective Knowledge Contributor

When carried to an extreme, presenting facts, figures, and technical knowledge to the group can backfire. The Ineffective Knowledge Contributor presents too much information for the team to digest and confuses team members with esoteric knowledge. He or she may also insist on documenting every opinion to the point that creativity and intuition will be discouraged. A favorite expression of the Ineffective Knowledge Contributor is, "Where's the data to support your position?" The Ineffective Knowledge Contributor may also attempt to dazzle team members with information technology when it's not appropriate.

Ineffective Collaborator

The Collaborator is willing to transcend her or his job description to help the team accomplish its mission. The Ineffective Collaborator pushes this too far by incessant insistence on meeting goals. He or she may be needlessly impatient with discussion that does not appear directly aimed at goal accomplishment. The biggest shortcoming of Ineffective Collaborators is that they attempt to interfere in the work of others, often to the point of rudeness. An example follows:

A diversity awareness task force was developed to find additional ways for the company to encourage an appreciation of diversity and to create more opportunities for a wider range of employees. During the second meeting, Stan agreed to bring in a laptop computer to take notes. Key points, along with statistical data, would be presented on a television monitor (hooked up to the laptop) in the room. Stan enjoyed this assignment because it represented a new challenge for him. Still on the upward part of his learning curve, Stan fumbled a little with the mechanics of the task.

Frank, a computer whiz, couldn't tolerate the fumbling. He insisted several times that he take over the controls because of his expertise. Stan replied good-naturedly that he wanted to attempt this challenging task. Frank kept pushing to take control of the computer apparatus to the point of disrupting the meeting. Stan finally told Frank, "Get out of my face! I volunteered first to scribe the meeting with my computer." [So much for a high-performing, high-morale team.]

Ineffective Supporter

The Supporter improves communication within the group by facilitating important processes, such as getting many people involved and resolving conflicts. The Ineffective Supporter becomes so caught up in process that he or she interferes with results. A teammate may reach a conclusion that other members accept as sound and are therefore willing to act on. The Ineffective Supporter might protest with the statement, "I have real concerns about how you reached your conclusion. You seem to have formed a subcommittee of one and therefore did not include group input. I move that we withhold approval on your decision until more people are involved."

The Ineffective Supporter can also consume more time than the group wants to commit to evaluating team process.

At one meeting the group was speeding toward reaching consensus on a key issue. Only ten minutes were left before several of the members had to depart for a flight. The Ineffective Supporter said, "We must stop now to evaluate our meeting. It's a necessary part of every well-run meeting." Several of the other team members brushed his comment aside and continued racing toward reaching consensus on the important decision.

Ineffective Challenger

A Challenger improves team functioning by asking enough critical questions to prevent groupthink and other forms of sloppy thinking. The Ineffective Challenger crosses into the danger zones of overemphasis on confrontation, abrasiveness, attacks, and belittling of teammates. Ineffective Challengers sometimes use the team meeting as a platform for attacking the larger organization and the boss. They believe erroneously that because a team is essentially a democratic form of organization, they have free rein to challenge authority. After too many disruptive challenges, the Ineffective Challenger is no longer taken seriously. The breakthrough team player has enough political smarts to avoid becoming an Ineffective Challenger.

Concealer

A Concealer enjoys the feeling of power that results from withholding information useful to other team members. His or her motive is to introduce this information when it would be the most advantageous, such as saving the team from a crisis. For example, a team leader might not tell the team about a contingency budget until the team has spent considerable time attempting to resolve the problem of depleted funds. The Concealer role can backfire. After his or her guise is exposed, team members may respond by keeping information from the Concealer. Consequently, all team members have difficulty getting their jobs accomplished.

Pessimist

A questioning, critical look at major issues facing the team is desirable. Yet some people drift into the dysfunctional role of the Pessimist. Such team members have a can't-do attitude and gripe and complain about almost every team assignment. Gradually the Pessimist's dour attitude drags down teammates, thus eroding team spirit and morale. The Pessimist role is incompatible with becoming a breakthrough team player.[5]

Squelcher

A bad role is to squelch team members when they are attempting to develop a point. Squelching can take many forms, including the following:

* Beginning to rebut a team member's point before he or she has finished speaking.
* Belittling a team member with a comment such as, "Where did that off-the-wall comment come from?"
* Attributing a comment to the person's functional background, with a statement such as, "What can you expect from a human-resources type?" or "Only an accountant would come up with that."
* Ignoring a team member's contribution, making him or her feel like a nonperson.

Squelching is absent from the breakthrough team player's tool kit. He or she has found more positive influence tactics, such as deftly complimenting positive contributions or asking for clarification on an illogical comment.

People Diagnoser

Another annoying and counterproductive role player is the person who labels others members of the team or diagnoses their motives. Although the labels and diagnoses contributed by the People Diagnoser may be correct, they make others defensive. As a result, productive communication may be thwarted. Here is an example of how labeling and diagnosing shuts off communication:

5. The Concealer and Pessimist roles are from a brochure published by Keye Productivity Center (Kansas City: American Management Association, 1994), p. 4.

Patrick has been speaking at length about how his department has been underbudgeted for many years. He describes several key projects his team had to forgo because of limited funds.

Marilyn, who disagrees that Patrick's department has been underfunded, lashes out: "Pat, if you didn't suffer from tunnel vision, you wouldn't say your department was underfunded. Instead, you would see that your group has received more than its fair share of the budget."

Patrick the spends ten minutes attempting to justify his conclusion. The progress of the meeting is halted, as Patrick feels compelled to prove that he does not suffer from tunnel vision.

Dominator

The best known team-subverting role is the Dominator, who attempts to seize control of the meeting. Although Dominators are often intelligent people who make incisive analyses of problems, their effectiveness is diminished by their behavior. Other team members soon come to think that the Dominator is more intent on having his or her way than in working collectively. Dominators are also annoying because they attempt to control the agenda, often instructing the group, "Okay, it's time to move off this point and move on to something else. We're getting nowhere." The Dominator may be right, but he or she wants to control the group too often.

Flaw-Finder

Some team members have an irresistible impulse to find flaws in the positions taken by other team members. The Flaw-Finder typically begins by making a positive statement about another team member's position, but finishes with a negative pronouncement. He or she qualifies all praise, often using the phrase "Yes, but. . . ." Representative Flaw-Finder statements include:

"I can see some merit in your argument, but it is based on a limited overall perspective."

"The material you prepared for the group is generally sound. However, your conclusion doesn't follow from the data."

Naysayer

More extreme than the Flaw-Finder is the person who disagrees with virtually every position taken by others without also pointing out its merits. The Naysayer is the devil's advocate who lets the group know clearly the deficiencies in every plan. In contrast, the Challenger criticizes only when he or she perceives a legitimate need to prevent the group from making a mistake.

The Naysayer is quick to point out that an idea won't work or that a proposal will not be accepted by the larger organization. The odds are in favor of the Naysayer being right many times, because most plans and proposals do have flaws. After awhile, however, a Naysayer's negativism becomes annoying.

A Method for Neutralizing
Team-Subverting Roles

Acting as a team member or a team leader, the breakthrough team player has an important stake in neutralizing the impact of people who subvert team efforts. If the subverters lower team productivity, the person attempting to become an outstanding team player will be associated with an unsuccessful team. In addition, a person who can stop a subverter in his or her tracks will be perceived as having excellent interpersonal skills.

The core method for preventing a potential subverter from hurting productivity and group spirit is to confront that person firmly at the time of the disruption. Several confrontations will usually be required to change the subverter's behavior. Here are two examples of the type of confrontation necessary to prevent a subverter from damaging team productivity and morale:

[SCENARIO 1]

A Squelcher on the team jumps in to make a point before you have finished your presentation. After the

Squelcher has finished, you intervene: "You jumped in with your point in the middle of my sentence. Is that because you weren't listening? Or is it because you didn't think what I had to say was important?" If the Squelcher interrupts somebody else, make a similar confrontation.

[SCENARIO 2]

A Flaw-Finder once again finds a flaw in a position taken by another team member. You respond: "I notice that you always find something terribly wrong with the output of another team member. Is this because you are trying to be helpful? Or is this just a game you are playing to put others down?"

The accompanying list will serve as a memory jogger about team-subverting roles. It is possible that one person may occupy several of these roles from time to time.

Team-Subverting Roles

- Ineffective Knowledge Contributor
- Ineffective Collaborator
- Ineffective Supporter
- Ineffective Challenger
- Concealer
- Pessimist
- Squelcher
- People Diagnoser
- Dominator
- Flaw-Finder
- Naysayer

Understanding the many different positive and negative roles possible in a team effort is an important prelude to another set of skills and knowledge required for outstanding team play. Today's breakthrough team player has effective cross-functional skills.

5

Developing Cross-Functional Skills

A key development in the new workplace is an emphasis on getting work accomplished in cross-functional teams. In a cross-functional team, people from different functions (or disciplines) pool their efforts to achieve a goal. The breakthrough team player therefore must be able to work effectively in teams composed of people with educations, training, fields of specialization, and perspectives different from his or her own.

Among the various types of cross-functional teams are product development teams, project teams, multidisciplinary task forces, and process teams. A process team is a group of people who work on a business process, such as getting a product to a customer. The process team stands in contrast to a traditional department responsible for building a product or performing one major activity.

All of the information presented so far about being an effective team player applies to performing well on a cross-functional team. Nevertheless, a cross-functional team has enough separate challenges to require an additional set of attitudes and skills to achieve breakthrough status. As a prelude to learning more details about cross-functional teams and cross-functional thinking, take the accompanying quiz. It is designed to help you measure your propensity toward cross-functional thinking.

Gauging Your Cross-Functional Thinking

Directions: Indicate the extent to which you agree or disagree with each of the following statements: strongly disagree (SD);

disagree (D); neutral (N); agree (A); strongly agree (SA). Circle the number under the most accurate answer for each question. If you have not experienced the situation described, imagine how you might think and act if placed in that situation.

	SD	D	N	A	SA
1. It is best to stick to your specialty and not comment about the work done by people from other disciplines.	5	4	3	2	1
2. I enjoy learning about the contribution made by other departments in my company.	1	2	3	4	5
3. I rarely talk to people on the job whose work is much different from mine.	5	4	3	2	1
4. When I take on an assignment for the company, I think first of how well the assignment will help my career.	5	4	3	2	1
5. An excellent philosophy is "It's not what your company can do for you, but what you can do for your company."	1	2	3	4	5
6. Getting people together from different specialties to discuss a technical problem is usually a waste of time.	5	4	3	2	1
7. The best business judgments are likely to come from talking over the problem with people from different departments or other units.	1	2	3	4	5
8. CEOs have limited perspectives because they no longer concentrate in one area of expertise.	5	4	3	2	1
9. Talking over business problems with people from different areas often leads to a superior solution.	1	2	3	4	5

	SD	D	N	A	SA

10. It would suit my interests to work almost exclusively with people doing the same type of work as me.   5   4   3   2   1

Total Score _____

Scoring and interpretation: Add the numbers you have circled to find your total score. Use the following information to interpret your score:

45–50   You have the right mental set to think cross-functionally on the job. This type of thinking will help you become a breakthrough team player on a cross-functional team.

25–44   You have an average tendency to think cross-functionally. Get more in the cross-functional thinking mode to do a better job on a cross-functional team.

10–24   You think primarily in functional terms. To be fully effective in the modern team structures you will have to broaden your outlook about the importance of cross-functional thinking.

The Nature of Cross-Functional Teams

Understanding the nature of a cross-functional team facilitates achieving breakthrough status. Furthermore, if you are to be a breakthrough team player in the changing workplace, you will need to spend considerable time as a member of cross-functional teams.

I emphasize cross-functional teams because they have proliferated in both private and public organizations. So much problem-solving takes place in multidisciplinary (a synonym for *cross-functional*) teams that business schools now offer many cross-functional learning experiences. Cross-functional teams are used in organizations for such purposes as:

- Developing new products
- Improving quality
- Empowering employees with more authority and responsibility
- Training employees in cultural diversity
- Reducing costs
- Making downsizing decisions
- Running a company (in the form of an executive team)

Today's cross-functional teams are an extension of yesterday's project teams (or groups). Projects are formed by placing together a group of people from different organizational units. Members are all committed to a specific purpose, such as designing a minivan or luxury airliner. Projects are also formed to construct buildings or make a movie.

Workplace innovations in the 1980s increased the need for cross-functional coordination. Total quality management and time-based competition (speed is the competitive advantage) required cross-functional thinking. Then came demands from top management for product design with a cross-functional perspective; products were to be designed for quality and ease of manufacturing.

In the 1990s, demands for designs that allowed products to be recycled without inordinate difficulty came from customers and top management. For example, "design for re-manufacturing" has been championed by Mercedes Benz. Mercedes cars are being designed to be dismantled (when their useful life is over) by salvage technicians and the parts readily recycled, instead of being melted down. The design team for a Mercedes would therefore include an auto-salvage specialist and an environmentalist.

Designing products with the requirements of another organizational unit in mind has another cross-functional consequence. The design of manufacturing methods, training programs, vendor selection, marketing strategies, and so forth, all occur simultaneously with the design of a product. Considerable coordination and decision making across functions is required to accomplish a simultaneous design project.

As a consequence of taking into account several key viewpoints, cross-functional teams for new product development have burgeoned. Approximately one-half of new product development teams have cross-functional membership. Organizations redesigning their work processes usually select new product development as a core process. As a result, the popularity of cross-functional teams has increased.

Charles Garfield, a psychologist and scientist on the Apollo 11 mission team, sheds additional light on the nature of cross-functional teams. He says that cross-functional teams can be built essentially by getting people from different functional areas into a room with a facilitator. The facilitator helps break down departmental barriers. Garfield questions the wisdom of having one department work for months, and then tossing its plan over the wall to another department. The problem is that a representative from the next department will often say, "That won't work!" To emphasize his or her point, the plan will be tossed back over the wall.

It is better to gather people from different functional areas to coordinate their efforts from the beginning, and then turn them loose. The facilitator or leader must trust the wisdom of the group. If you are the leader, contribute your views but act mostly to reconcile conflicting opinions.[1]

Advantages of Cross-Functional Teams

Cross-functional teams have several notable advantages, all of which have contributed to their popularity. Being aware of these advantages can help you direct the team toward achieving them.

Speed

A major advantage of cross-functional teams is speed. The teams enhance communication across groups, which often leads to saving money by reducing product development time. If you per-

1. "Talking With Dr. Charles Garfield About Empowering Your Team," *Working Smart* (June 1992), p. 7.

form well on a product development team you therefore might be able to share some glory.

In 1988, AT&T began developing a cordless telephone. John Hanley, the vice president of product development, hoped to reduce product development time by 50 percent. He knew the company would have to make major changes to accomplish this goal. A major obstacle the company faced was a tightly formed hierarchical structure. In the past, the AT&T approach to product development resembled a relay system: The product development group would hand a design over to manufacturing. Next, manufacturing would hand the product over to marketing to sell to consumers.

Hanley revamped the process by forming teams whose membership included engineers, manufacturers, and marketers. Team members were granted the authority to decide how much the product would cost, how it would work, and its appearance. Rigid speed requirements were established before design requirements were fixed.

Partly because they did not have to send decisions up the hierarchy for approval, the team achieved tight deadlines. As a result of the shift to cross-functional teams, AT&T cut development time from two years down to one year. Equally significant, the manufacturing cost was lowered and product quality improved.[2]

An important implication of the case history just presented is that to be a breakthrough cross-functional team member you have to relish speed. Many teams are slow-moving, time-consuming, heel-dragging, action-delaying mechanisms. In contrast, most product development, cross-functional teams are established to achieve rapid results.

2. Based on information in D. Keith Denton, "Multi-Skilled Teams Replace Old Work Systems," *HRMagazine* (September 1992), p. 49.

Ability to Solve Complex Problems

Proper use of cross-functional teams helps the organization solve complex problems.[3] Since most complex problems involve many disciplines, a cross-functional team is best for dealing with them. You can contribute to solving complex problems by having expertise in your own area combined with a willingness to accept the contribution of people from other disciplines. Designing a new home entertainment system, for example, would require contributions from several disciplines including electronics engineering, interior design, and ergonomics (making machines fit human requirements).

Customer Focus

Cross-functional teams improve an organization's ability to focus on customer requirements. One department or one person cannot know all these requirements. By members from several different organizational units working together, customer requirements can be better understood.

Creativity

A potential contribution of a heterogeneous team is creative solutions to problems. In a cross-functional team, the creativity comes about as different perspectives are brought to bear on a problem. You can enhance your creativity as a member of a cross-functional team if you open yourself to intellectual stimulation by different perspectives.

Michelin Tires developed a new line of snow tires that proved to be successful. Part of the success was attributed to a marketing specialist on the team who emphasized that many of the people who use snow tires actually

3. This and the next three points are based on Glenn M. Parker, *Cross-Functional Teams: Working With Allies, Enemies, and Other Strangers* (San Francisco: Jossey-Bass, 1994), pp. 11–29.

enjoy snow. They would want a product that celebrated the beauty of snow. As a consequence, the new tire was called *Pnu Alpin* (French for "alpine tire," thus making a connection between alpine skiing and the Michelin snow tire).

Single Point of Contact for Information

In a typical functional form of organization, a large, long-term project moves from one department to another. Each department is working on a separate piece of the larger entity, such as various departments contributing different components of a home entertainment center. When a cross-functional team is assembled, the team becomes the contact point for all information about the status of the project. A breakthrough team player enjoys communicating with outsiders about the status of the project and giving out other information.

Using a Cross-Functional Team to Reengineer Work

Cross-functional teams can be used to streamline or reengineer work. The AT&T experience with the cordless telephone was an example of this application. Syntex Inc., the giant pharmaceutical company, used cross-functional teams explicitly to simplify work.

In 1991, Syntex recognized that the pharmaceutical industry was facing substantial change. The company decided it would have to become more innovative and efficient to bring products to market more quickly than was done previously. Developing a new drug can cost more than $250 million and take ten years to complete. The introduction of a new drug also requires leading-edge technology to establish the accuracy of clinical trials and the hundreds of thousands of pages of data resulting from the trials.

Syntex responded at first by purchasing state-of-the-art computers and information systems to track and verify the volumes of data. But then according to Liz Davila, vice president of quality and reengineering at Syntex, the company learned about reengineering. In her words, "We realized that the systems must be designed around the business processes. It became clear that we needed to make fundamental changes in the way we work. We needed to take a step back and reexamine every process associated with drug development before we could install the technology."

After examining the company structure and its work processes, the company found that scientists, clinical specialists, legal experts, regulatory affairs specialists, and marketing specialists did not integrate well across departmental lines. Many of these people worked in isolation, and considerable time was lost in shuffling paper between desks. Another point of confusion and error was that many specialists had to keep track of several projects at a time.

Syntex went the reengineering route to conquer its work process problems. Cross-functional teams were created of eight to twelve members, each assigned to a particular project. Team members would retain expertise in their particular disciplines. Yet they would also acquire enough general knowledge that they could handle inquiries from inside and outside the company. Response time was reduced, partially by eliminating the delay caused by voice mail and e-mail messages that previously had to wait for a particular individual to respond.

Syntex today has twelve cross-functional teams in its drug development division. "As we got more involved we became even bolder," says Davila. "We realized there are far more opportunities to reduce work and eliminate handoffs than we ever imagined." Syntex expects to reduce development time and costs by 20 percent.

Cross-functional team members at Syntex have enjoyed the challenges of working with each other, although most of them previously worked primarily with people from their own discipline. The team members took pride in the fact that by working in cross-functional groups they have enabled the company to become more productive.[4]

A key lesson from the Syntex experience is that being a member of a cross-functional team can enhance one's reputation for productivity. Should you become a member of a cross-functional team, let others in the organization know how effective you and your teammates have been.

Personal Attributes of the Cross-Functional Team Player

An effective cross-functional team player has most of the attributes of effective leaders, managers, professionals, and team players in general. All of the actions and attributes described in Chapter 2 about the consummate team player also apply to a cross-functional team. In addition, there are other intellectual and personality factors that seem especially important for high performance on a cross-functional team. All of these attributes can be improved with self-discipline, practice, and training.

Having the right attributes is especially important when working on a cross-functional team. Your teammates may readily accept your technical expertise because they are outsiders to your field. However, you will probably have a harder time selling them on your viewpoint than you would with people from your own discipline.

Self-Confidence

You would be hard pressed to find a demanding work situation in which self-confidence was not important for success. Self-confidence is especially important to a member of a cross-functional team, because he or she is working with people from other disciplines who may challenge the relevance of your specialty. Tricia,

4. Adapted from Samuel Greengard, "Reengineering: Out of the Rubble," *Personnel Journal* (December 1993), pp. 48H-48K.

a social worker assigned to a cross-functional team in a hospital, said:

> The other members of the team patronized me at first. They had the attitude that social work isn't very important in a hospital setting. I had to fight for the right to be accepted as a fully contributing member of the team.

Assertiveness

Being forthright in expressing your demands, opinions, feelings, and attitudes is important for most of the same reasons as self-confidence. You cannot be timid if you want to sell your perspective to others in a cross-functional team. A smooth-running cross-functional team cannot be a battleground in which members from various disciplines fight for air time. Nevertheless, if you do not make your points explicit, your potential contribution can be overlooked.

Sense of Humor

Since a cross-functional team can be a demanding, tension-filled situation, an effective use of humor is an important part of the role of the team leader and the team player. Humor relieves tension, lessens conflict, and raises team spirit within the group. The most sophisticated use of humor for a breakthrough team player, however, is to make a point and influence others.

At a consumer electronics company, a quality-improvement team was formed with members from several functions. A major problem facing the company was the high number of products brought back for warranty work. Ratings for customer service, however, were consistently positive. The team began formulating tactics for dealing with the problem. Karl, a marketing specialist, said he had a temporary solution to the problem. He recommended that the company run an advertising campaign based on the theme "We may not get things right the first time. But not to worry. We take back defective products with a smile.'' [*Karl's comment underscored in a nice way the urgency of the challenge facing the group.*]

High Tolerance for Frustration

Cross-functional teams are often selected to take on formidable tasks such as preventing and correcting product defects, redesigning work processes, or developing a new product. The team may become frustrated if it doesn't accomplish its objectives as quickly as the members would like or if the developed plan may not be as elegant as they had hoped. A less well-known source of frustration facing many cross-functional teams is that their recommendations are ignored by top management. This is particularly frustrating when the group has worked for a long time to prepare a complicated report with dozens of recommendations.

The executive or executives who formed the team may reject the recommendations for several reasons. First, the recommendations may clash with the course of action top management wanted to take. Second, top management may have lost interest in the project. Third, the cross-functional team may have been formed just to placate employees who thought that top management did not believe in empowerment. Whatever the reason, team members need to be able to deal with the frustration that will result.

Sensitivity to Others

To function effectively on a cross-functional team, each person should be able to understand the other members' interests and attitudes, and how to capture their attention. Sensitivity to others is obviously important in all types of groups, but the cross-discipline team requires extra sensitivity. The challenge is to show a sincere interest in the viewpoints of people with a substantially different orientation than your own. One area where such sensitivity is called for is the potential clash in viewpoints between people from technical versus nontechnical disciplines.

Cross-functional team members from engineering and information technology may be quick to dismiss the contribution of members from marketing or human resources as being simply common sense. Members from marketing and human resources may in turn be insensitive to representatives of engineering and information technology, complaining that they overlook the human element in a problem. The breakthrough team player is able to appreciate the contribution of team members from all disciplines.

Flexibility

The ability to adjust to different situations is another key attribute for successful performance on cross-functional teams. Flexible team players are able to adjust to the demands of different situations, much like antilock brakes enable an automobile to adjust to changes in road conditions. Cross-functional team members often shift back and forth between working in their regular functional groups and on the team.

A breakthrough member of a cross-functional team needs to be flexible for another major reason. He or she is required to shift away from thinking functionally and toward thinking cross-functionally. Jennifer, a marketing specialist, expressed the shift in these terms:

> Before I was assigned to the multidisciplinary product development team, I was heavily marketing-oriented. My attitude was that without effective marketing, the manufacturing group would be making scrap. I also felt that without marketing, people like accountants and human resources specialists would be unemployed. My attitude hasn't changed 100 percent [*she laughs*], but I now realize we are all part of a total system. No one part of the system is more important than others, just like every part of a motor makes a contribution. Without the fan, the pistons will grind to a halt.

The importance of openness to new ideas for being a consummate team player was described in Chapter 2. Being open to new ideas and perspectives is another manifestation of the need for flexibility on the part of the breakthrough team player.

Developing a Cross-Functional Perspective

The bedrock skill required for outstanding performance on a cross-functional team is to develop a cross-functional perspective. The team leader as well as team members must learn to literally think across functions for the good of the total organization. Each team member must think like a general manager, CEO, or statesman. What is good for the total organization is good for each organizational unit. The business cliché of the mid-1990s has merit here. You must forget about your functional silos.

Another way of framing the same issue is that a key factor in working effectively on a cross-functional team is to look at problems from a broad, or multidisciplinary, perspective. Visualize the following scenario:

You are asked to investigate customer complaints that your product is too expensive. Functional viewpoints of the problem are as follows:

- Finance must find a way to lower the cost. Costs are obviously out of line.
- Manufacturing must squeeze some more cost out of the product. (Maybe you can buy lower-priced components and cut down on overtime.)
- Marketing must find a way to explain why this product is a bargain at its present price.
- Engineering must incorporate a new high-tech feature that will dazzle customers and make them forget about price.

A person with cross-functional skills will encourage team members to look at several perspectives in resolving the problem. For the cross-functional perspective, the team has a *business* problem—not a finance, marketing, manufacturing, or engineering problem.

Another component of cross-functional skills is the ability to relate comfortably to people from different disciplines. To relate comfortably, a person must overcome many stereotypes about other functions. Stereotypes may have some validity; yet they block communication by other team members of potential contributions. Here are a few of these stereotypes:

* Marketing people care much more about sales volume and market share than earning a profit.
* Finance people just don't understand that you have to spend money to make money.
* Manufacturing people care mostly about achieving an orderly flow of work; customer needs are of much less concern to them.
* Human resources people are much more concerned about job satisfaction than profits.
* Engineering people are into technology, gadgetry, bells and whistles, and quality at any price. They are much less concerned about delivering products of interest to customers.

The team player with effective cross-functional skills understands the perspectives of the various disciplines. He or she uses empathy to help find common interests and build bridges across disciplines. A finance specialist assigned to a quality improvement team made this comment with respect to resolving a customer complaint about price: "I don't care whose ox gets gored. Let's satisfy the customer and make some money at the same time."

Developing a cross-functional perspective can be approached in several ways, all centering around the idea of shedding the functional viewpoint. Several additional suggestions follow:

* *Keep in mind the venerable analogy about wearing different hats.* Think about owning a functional hat and a cross-functional

hat. Choose which hat to wear on a given day. When you are doing work for the cross-functional team, wear your cross-functional hat.

Remember that casting aside the functional hat is difficult for most people. Terry Ennis, a DuPont executive, says, "It's very unsettling and threatening for people. You find line and functional managers who have been honored and rewarded for what they've done for decades. You're in a white-water zone when you change."[5]

• *Imagine that you are a general manager.* You can stimulate your cross-functional thinking by imagining yourself as a general manager facing the problem at hand.

You are a member of a process redesign team. The team is about to recommend eliminating outside sales representatives for a particular product line. From a self-interested point of view, the marketing representative would ordinarily think, "There goes the outside sales group right out the door." The human resources representative might say, "There goes my program for recruiting, selecting, and training outside sales representatives."

To keep self-interested, functional thinking from snowballing, you say, "Let's look at our redesign plan as if we were all general managers. What redesign solutions will benefit the organization as a whole? For now, let's forget about which functional group will take the biggest hit. What counts is the long-term health of the entire organization."

• *Take advantage of any opportunity for multidisciplinary training.* An elegant way to develop cross-functional thinking is to participate in multifunctional development. Such development is usually reserved for managers, but professional and technical workers sometimes participate. Multifunctional development is an intentional effort to enhance the capacity of selected individuals by exposing them to various functions within an organiza-

5. Quoted in John A. Byrne, "The Horizontal Corporation: It's About Managing Across, Not Up and Down," *Business Week* (December 20, 1993), p. 79.

tion. Any opportunity along these lines that you can grab will help you think cross-functionally. Furthermore, it will help groom you for promotion. A fundamental truth about vertical mobility is that broad experience enhances promotability.

The various types of multifunctional managerial development have been ranked in terms of the intensity of the experience and commitment by the organization. In descending order, the experiences are:

1. Complete mobility across organizational functions (the type of experience given fast-trackers)
2. Temporary assignments (from six months to two years) outside the person's home function
3. Exposure to other functions on task forces, project teams, and cross-functional teams
4. Classroom education about other functions

If the organization does not make such developmental experiences available to you, engage in self-study through reading and participation in seminars. After you feel confident that you have acquired cross-functional breadth, inform key organizational members of your progress.

Resolving Conflict Within the Cross-Functional Team

Conflict frequently takes place within cross-functional teams, because people with different perspectives, skills, and values are placed in close psychological and physical proximity. Harmony is not a natural state for a heterogeneous group. Conflicts that occur within the team offer the advantage of triggering people into presenting their views with more clarity and precision. Creative problem-solving is often the result. Conflict can also be beneficial because it points toward issues that remain to be resolved.

A representative example of the nature of the conflict often found in a cross-functional team took place at a manufacturer of office equipment.

A multidisciplinary task force was formed to develop a companywide perspective on quality improvement. Representatives from the major functions of the business were assigned to the task force, including a manager from public communications.

During the first several meetings, each member emphasized how his or her function could make a major contribution to quality improvement. The representative from manufacturing described how the biggest quality challenge would be to reduce variability in manufacturing. The representative from customer service explained that courteous and prompt servicing of customer machines carried considerable weight in projecting a quality image. Tension mounted as each representative attempted to sell the other team members on the importance of his or her function's contribution to quality.

The last person to present was Dan, the representative from public communications. He contended that the public communications group had the best perspective on quality. Dan argued that public communications was the one function committed to serving *all* the customers. His argument was that the government, public interest groups, suppliers, and so forth, should be considered customers in a new meaning of the term. Only by maintaining the highest ethics could the company become a high-quality organization. He concluded that ethics training should therefore be a central part of quality improvement.

Kristen, the accounting and finance representative, was skeptical and expressed his reservations about Dan's version of quality improvement. Derrick, the engineering representative, slammed down his notepad in disgust. "Why in the world do our people need ethics training? It's all common sense. If our employees need to know more about ethics, they can attend Bible school at night."

Dan then tore into Derrick about his insensitivity to one of the most important issues of the day. Two group meetings were spent arguing about whether ethics training should be included in training for quality. A compromise was finally reached of including thirty minutes of ethics training in a quality-improvement course. No member of the team was truly satisfied with the solution, but the issue was put to rest.

To be a breakthrough team player on a cross-functional team, you will need to apply your knowledge about conflict resolution. Debates and barely acceptable compromises will not do. Instead, you will have to use more sophisticated approaches to resolving conflict. A description of several methods of conflict resolution is outside the scope of this book. Nevertheless, here is one method most applicable to the situation.

The conflict that takes place in cross-functional teams is generally motivated by the belief that one's position is right, and not by a mean-spirited attitude or an attempt to hurt the others. The general-purpose conflict-resolution technique called confrontation and problem-solving is therefore recommended.

The ideal approach to resolving any conflict is to confront the real issue, and then solve the problem. Your goal is to identify the underlying facts, logic, or emotions that account for your differences with another person on the team. Confrontation can proceed gently in a way that preserves a good working relationship.

Let's get back to Dan and Derrick on the quality-improvement task force. Dan is angry with Derrick because he is belittling the contribution of ethics to high quality. Dan becomes so enraged that he tears into Derrick, thus damaging their working relationship and probably not resolving the conflict. Dan might have fared better if he had confronted Derrick in this manner:

Dan: Derrick, your position is that ethics is only common sense, so we don't need to train our staff in ethics.
Derrick: Yes, I said that because I meant it.
Dan: I guess the real issue here is that we disagree on the training our people need. You could be right that much of what we call ethics is common sense.
Derrick: I'm glad you agree that I could be right.
Dan: My big concern is that even if ethics is common sense, too many business people aren't using their common sense about ethics. I read about ethical violations in business al-

most every day. I guess you could say we need to train people how to apply their common sense about ethics to a
business situation. We could then satisfy a greater number
of our constituents.
Derrick: Now I see your point more clearly.

This chapter focused on skills important to working successfully in cross-functional teams. The next chapter shifts to a
set of generic skills for any team setting: political skills.

6

Political Tactics for Team Players

Breakthrough team players have outstanding interpersonal skills. They gain the cooperation of people over whom they lack formal authority, they resolve workplace conflict, and they take over the leadership reins when necessary. To accomplish these demanding interpersonal tasks, breakthrough players need considerable political skill. The breakthrough team player must therefore be an adept office politician.

You might be concerned that being an *office politician* clashes with the spirit of cooperation and mutual respect that is supposed to be part of a high-performing, team-based organization. Such concern has merit, but it does not override three important reasons for being a good team politician. First, this definition of politics does not refer to unethical, devious behavior. As used here, politics is the art of using informal influence tactics to gain for yourself an important advantage such as more power or fair treatment. To be political is to know how to get an equitable share of power flowing in your direction.

A second justification for being political is that the modern team-based organization is not the highly ethical, high-minded, altruistic environment that many executives and management experts contend it is. A substantial proportion of people still scramble for power, recognition, and resources. You have to be political to get your share of resources and to counterattack the self-centeredness of others.

A third justification for being a good team politician is that because teammates can have an important impact on your future, you need to gain their support. Input by teammates is playing an increasingly important role in performance evaluation and salary increases. In years past, it was primarily the boss and your boss's boss whom you had to please to get an above-average performance appraisal. Today, teammates also have to be cultivated. A growing number of organizations, including units within Xerox Corporation, use a formal system of performance evaluation by peers.

As a starting point in our analysis of team politics, take the accompanying quiz. It will help you gain insight into your current status as an effective political player at the team level.

The Team Politics Questionnaire

Directions: Respond to the following statements as they relate to your team experience. If you have never worked on a team, on or off the job, imagine how you would act or think if you were a team member. Indicate the extent to which you agree or disagree with each of the following statements: strongly agree (SA); agree (A); neutral (N); disagree (D); strongly disagree (SD). Circle the number under the most accurate answer for each question.

	SA	A	N	D	SD
1. I would ask a teammate's opinion on personal matters even if I didn't need the advice, just to show that I respected his or her judgment.	5	4	3	2	1
2. I would help a team member with a household chore on a Sunday afternoon.	5	4	3	2	1
3. I would invite a teammate to a party in my home, even if I didn't like him or her.	5	4	3	2	1
4. I would compliment teammates only when it was strictly deserved.	1	2	3	4	5
5. When not in a team meeting, I would make no special effort to interact with teammates.	1	2	3	4	5

	SA	A	N	D	SD
6. I would be willing to start negative rumors about a rival teammate.	5	4	3	2	1
7. Given a choice, I would only take on assignments within the team that would make me look good.	5	4	3	2	1
8. I would never tell a teammate anything that he or she could conceivably use against me in the future.	5	4	3	2	1
9. On occasion, I would surprise the team by bringing donuts or bagels and cream cheese to a meeting.	5	4	3	2	1
10. I would not try to impress my teammates. It's better to let my good work speak for itself.	1	2	3	4	5
11. I would try to be as nice as possible to all my teammates, even if I didn't like a particular person.	5	4	3	2	1
12. I would attend a team picnic just to be seen, even if I had something more important to do that day.	5	4	3	2	1
13. The best way to impress people would be to tell them what they want to hear.	5	4	3	2	1
14. I would attempt to give each team member a sincere compliment at least once a month.	5	4	3	2	1
15. I would not "kiss up" to the team leader.	1	2	3	4	5
16. I would work late in the office just to impress my teammates.	5	4	3	2	1
17. I would share my expertise with teammates, even though it might mean that I no longer had a technical edge over them.	1	2	3	4	5

	SA	A	N	D	SD
18. I would readily adapt to the jargon of the team, just so I fitted right in with the group.	5	4	3	2	1
19. When time was at a premium, I would put aside politeness toward team members.	1	2	3	4	5
20. I would recommend a highly competent person for membership on our team even if I thought that person would outshine me.	1	2	3	4	5
21. I would ask other team members' advice even if I didn't intend to use their input.	5	4	3	2	1
22. I would specifically let my teammates know that I was available for them when they needed my help.	5	4	3	2	1
23. Whenever I could do it tactfully, I would let other members of the team know of my accomplishments.	5	4	3	2	1
24. It would not be unusual for me to do a favor for a teammate even if I was not concerned about getting the favor returned at a later time.	1	2	3	4	5
25. I think flattering teammates is a waste of time.	1	2	3	4	5

Total score _____

Scoring and interpretation: Calculate your total score by adding up the numbers that you circled. Your score provides an approximate guide to your tendencies toward playing team politics (office politics directed specifically at winning favor as a team member)

100–125   You are going too far in playing team politics. Being this political could lead to the perception that you are insincere and much too concerned about self-advancement at the expense of the

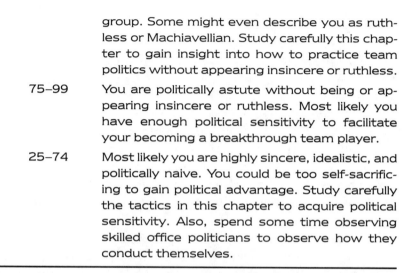

group. Some might even describe you as ruthless or Machiavellian. Study carefully this chapter to gain insight into how to practice team politics without appearing insincere or ruthless.

75–99   You are politically astute without being or appearing insincere or ruthless. Most likely you have enough political sensitivity to facilitate your becoming a breakthrough team player.

25–74   Most likely you are highly sincere, idealistic, and politically naive. You could be too self-sacrificing to gain political advantage. Study carefully the tactics in this chapter to acquire political sensitivity. Also, spend some time observing skilled office politicians to observe how they conduct themselves.

The purpose of this chapter is to describe ethical political tactics for winning the support of teammates. The tactics are classified into two categories: tactics for building relationships, and tactics aimed directly at influencing others to your way of thinking. All of the political tactics presented here are designed to supplement, not substitute for, good job performance. The skilled team politician establishes a reputation for high performance before consciously attempting to use political techniques for building relationships and influencing others.

Tactics for Building Relationships With Teammates

For a privileged few team players, building good relationships with teammates is an intuitive process. They are able to win the support of team members without planning and conscious effort. The majority of team players, however, would benefit from a more deliberate approach to cultivating others on the team. Even if you have finely tuned intuition for relationship building, you might benefit from a careful look at the tactics described next. You never know where there is an approach not already in your repertoire.

Display Unbridled Enthusiasm

The breakthrough team player is consistently enthusiastic in the factory, mill, laboratory, or office. He or she is visibly excited about team projects, assignments, and results. Laughter and body language can be key signals of enthusiasm. Enthusiasm helps build relationships with teammates because you become a source of inspiration and you elevate team spirit.

Enthusiasm works as a relationship builder for another important reason. An enthusiastic person is perceived as cooperative, and cooperation is virtually synonymous with teamwork.

Sheila, a member of the data management department in her company, was selected as a supervisor well ahead of her turn (based on seniority). When asked why Sheila was promoted so rapidly to supervisor, her manager said: "Sheila quickly developed a reputation as the gung-ho person in the group. When others griped about a heavy workload, Sheila was there with a smile encouraging others to dig in. We need someone like Sheila as the supervisor. Who wants a deadpan?"

Put Your Team's Goals Before Your Own

If you weren't interested in your career goals and in advancing your own cause, you probably wouldn't be reading this book. Instead, you would be reading information aimed more directly at managing others and worrying about their welfare. Here is where a paradox enters the picture. To gain the cooperation of teammates, you must look for ways to put your team's goals before your own. By occasionally putting the team first, you will be recognized as an excellent team player. In turn, your cause will be advanced because your reputation is enhanced.

An analogy can be drawn with empowerment. When the manager transfers power to group members, the group soon gains more power. Since the group now has more power, it can accomplish more. As the group accomplishes more, the manager is considered more powerful. Furthermore, the manager can work on other tasks (that may lead to more power), because the group has now assumed more of the manager's responsibilities.

Opportunities to put the team's goals before your own do not occur every workweek. You need to stay keenly perceptive to look for the right opening. Here are two examples: •

1. The team decides to hold an all-day Saturday retreat to hammer out a new mission statement. You have already made plans for a vacation with your family the same weekend as the retreat. During a meeting you announce to the group that you have switched your plans because of the importance of the mission statement.

2. You have been on a project for one year that is now phasing down. Being a survivalist, you locate yourself a position on another company project that is scheduled to start in one month. You explain your situation to your present project leader, who understands your predicament. She pleads with you to wait until this project is complete because the team needs you. After careful consideration of the team's needs (and your desire to preserve your good-person reputation), you decide to delay joining the new team. Next, you casually mention your decision to your teammates. Word quickly spreads of your good deed, and your team player reputation is strengthened.

Use Team-Oriented Language

A subtle, yet high-impact, tactic of team politics is to use words and phrases that indicate you have a strong team orientation. *Team-oriented language* refers to expressions that emphasize or reinforce the importance of teamwork. Use your imagination to develop team-oriented language of your own that adroitly fits your situation. A general guide is to emphasize the words *we* and *us*, rather than *I, mine,* and *me.* As a starter, consider the following specific phrases:

"Let's play to win on this challenge."
"We had a wonderful week."
"If we all carry out our roles, I know we can win."
"It's tough to lose, but I know it won't break our team spirit."

"This has been a great team effort."
"Without you fellows, I would never have closed the deal."
"Let's all break bread together soon."

Involve Teammates in Conflict Resolution

A sophisticated tactic to showcase your dedication to team play is to involve teammates in resolving conflict. According to JoDell Steuver, too often when team members find themselves in conflict they try to go it alone rather seek help from other team members. Problems are created when one team member does not let others know what is happening. Too many people feel that seeking help in resolving conflicts is a sign of weakness.[1]

By letting teammates know when you need assistance, you have access to more ways of solving your problem. For example, if you were attempting to resolve a problem with a manager from another department, a team member might think of an approach that could help you. Sharing your problem with a teammate also has a political advantage. Your behavior says implicitly, "I trust your judgment to help me with a difficult problem."

Ask for Technical Help

Asking for help in solving problems between people offers an opportunity for political gain. Asking for technical assistance can also be a relationship builder within the team. As stated before, asking a person for assistance implies you respect his or her judgment, which in turn is a relationship builder. Paul, a member of a laboratory team, found that asking for help enabled him to build a relationship with a difficult-to-reach team member.

Paul was becoming frustrated with the e-mail system because it lacked the advanced functions ordinarily associated with word processing. For example, similar to most

1. Quoted in "Creating an Atmosphere of Trust," *Supervisory Management* (September 1994), p. 9.

e-mail systems, it did not allow for moving paragraphs around or electronic spell checking. Paul had heard that Diane, one of the least popular members of the team, knew how to load a word processing program into e-mail. He sent Diane an electronic message asking for her assistance. Diane responded with step-by-step instructions for merging WordPerfect into e-mail. After a few tries, Paul combined his e-mail with WordPerfect.

In addition to learning a valuable skill, Paul now had one more ally on the team. He cultivated the new relationship by asking Diane to join him for lunch. During team meetings, Paul found that Diane was quick to support his position.

Recognize the Accomplishments of Team Members

A pervasive human need is to achieve recognition. If you can learn to comfortably and genuinely recognize the accomplishments of teammates, your reputation will be enhanced. An important guideline is to make the recognition appropriate to the magnitude of the good deed. A member of a two-person sales team brought in an account that was difficult to attain. His teammate bought him a T-shirt with the inscription "World-Class Sales Rep." The representative responded, "I appreciate the thought, but I get the impression that you are patronizing me."

Show Concern About the Personal Problems of Coworkers

A straightforward human relations tactic for building good relationships with team members is to show concern for their personal problems and misfortunes. Find the right balance between morbid curiosity and snooping versus a genuine display of concern. If you show sincere concern for the adversity faced by a peer, you will help strengthen the bond between the two of you. If you learn that one of your teammates is going through the trauma of separation, offer your emotional support. Approach the person delicately and sincerely, and express your interest in the two of you getting together for dinner. Dinner is often better than lunch because a person traumatized by separation may need more time than a lunch break to talk about the problem.

While discussing your teammate's adversity, maintain a listening posture. Ask general questions, such as "How do you feel about the situation?" rather than pointed questions about details of the problem. Your beleaguered teammate will benefit because of the opportunity to vent feelings. Your gain—aside from helping a person in need—will be that you have developed one more ally on the team.

Appeal to Your Teammates' Personal Interests

A basic sales technique is to be familiar with the personal interests of your customers and then appeal to those interests before making a sales presentation. Similarly, managers are advised to relate to the interests of group members. The same technique works well in cultivating relationships with coworkers. It is especially impressive for a teammate to appeal to one's personal interests, because such behavior is expected more from sales people and managers.

Just as a sales representative does, maintain files on your teammates, either manual or computerized. Track important and obscure facts about each and mention these interests or ask questions about them at appropriate times. An example:

> MANDI ROBBINS
> Single, usually has new boyfriend every several months. Has cat named Roscoe. Prefers to talk about professional matters than chitchat during work time. Mother in precarious health; father very depressed. Vegetarian and animal rights activist. Rolling Stones fan and bicyclist. Politically liberal.

Update your files periodically. Keeping them current minimizes the mistake of asking about the health of a parent who died six months ago or about a relationship that no longer exists. The updated file system also helps you avoid the faux pas of calling a team member's spouse by the name of the coworker's former spouse at a party.

Be Patient and Tolerant

Patience and tolerance with teammates helps build good relationships because such treatment makes people feel more secure. The process works in this manner: A teammate asks you a question about the new vacation schedule, because he does not fully understand its implications. If he did understand it, he wouldn't be asking you the question. You begin to explain the implications of the schedule, and he is still confused. You become impatient at his lack of comprehension. Your impatience makes him tense, which further impairs his ability to understand the policy. If you are patient, perhaps he can overcome the block that is preventing him from understanding the policy. The following case history provides more details about the political use of patience and tolerance.

Five software engineers were working on the software for an image-editing product. Four people had been working on the product since its beginning. Cynthia, another software engineer, joined the group after about one year. She said that each of the four engineers who had been there before her were very helpful. However, she was most impressed by Stan: "Stan never seemed to tire of my questions even if they were basic. He was always willing to stop what he was doing to help me.

"In several instances Stan had to explain things to me numerous times before it finally registered. He never lost his patience. I don't think I could have made it without Stan's help. He was a real inspiration."

Stan's patience and understanding benefited him also. Helping develop the professional skills of another person is an inherently pleasant activity and is therefore self-rewarding. Also, Stan now created a strong ally whom he can count on in the future as needed.

Be a Diplomat

Another way of winning favor with team members is to avoid negative confrontations. Skillful use of diplomacy may enable you to maintain a positive image.

Teammates who irritate you are rarely doing it on purpose. Tactful actions on your part can sometimes take care of these annoyances without your having to confront the problem. Close your door, for example, if noisy teammates are gathered outside. If a teammate is consuming too much time in your office or cubicle, stand up. This serves as a nonverbal hint that it is time for your guest to leave, but it does not come across as pushy.

Sometimes subtlety does not work, and it may be necessary to diplomatically confront the annoying coworker. An effective approach is to precede a criticism with a compliment. Here is an example of this approach: "You're one of the most interesting and well-informed team members. Yet I just don't have the time during working hours to discuss so many worldly topics. Maybe we could save some of these conversations for after hours."

The accompanying list will help you review the tactics for building relationships with teammates. Next, we describe tactics for more directly getting people over to your side.

Building Relationships With Teammates

- Display unbridled enthusiasm.
- Put your team's goals before your own.
- Use team-oriented language.
- Involve teammates in conflict resolution.
- Recognize the accomplishments of team members.
- Show concern about the personal problems of coworkers.
- Appeal to your teammates' personal interests.
- Be patient and tolerant.
- Be a diplomat.

Tactics for Directly Influencing Teammates

The political tactics described so far are aimed at building relationships with teammates. Relationship builders are a major component of team politics, yet direct influence tactics must sometimes be used to accomplish your ends. Influence tactics are part of team politics because they are aimed at acquiring power by means other than strictly merit. Here we describe essentially ethical and honest influence tactics in keeping with the spirit of teamwork.

Rational Persuasion

The traditional way of influencing people through rational persuasion is still an important tactic and has relevance for dealing with teammates. Rational persuasion involves using logical arguments and factual evidence to convince another person that a proposal is workable and likely to achieve its goal. Assertiveness combined with careful research is necessary to make rational persuasion an effective tactic.

Rational persuasion is likely to be most effective with people who are intelligent and rational. You might be in a situation in which you want your teammate's support for a work-method improvement you think will help the group and contribute to your status as a breakthrough team player. The smartest people on your team are likely to be the most influential, so you want to sell them first on the merits of your idea. Rather than attempt to use an emotional appeal such as team pride, carefully specify why your work-method change is so valuable. Point to benefits such as reduced cycle time, cost savings, and quality improvement.

Exchange Favors and Strike a Bargain

Offering to exchange favors if a teammate will help you achieve a work goal is another standard influence tactic. The exchange often translates into one person being willing to reciprocate at a later date. The exchange might also be promising a share of the benefits if your teammate helps you accomplish a task. For example, you might promise to place a teammate's name on a report to top management if that person helps analyze the data and prepare the tables.

Another perspective on exchange and bargaining is that you are building a favor bank. In other words, you do favors for people today with the expectation that you can make a withdrawal from the favor bank when needed. Your teammate may prefer not to make an out-of-town trip to cover a customer emergency, because it conflicts with a pressing family obligation. You might make the trip for your teammate. He now "owes you one." Furthermore, you have strengthened your relationship with him.

Legitimizing a Request

To legitimize is to verify that an influence attempt is within the influencer's scope of authority. Another aspect of legitimizing is to show that your request for help is consistent with organizational policies, practices, and expectations of professional people. Making legitimate requests is an effective influence tactic because most workers are willing to comply with regulations.

As a team member, you can thus exert influence with a statement such as this one: "I've been asked by the vice president of finance to be the team representative for finding ways to reduce expenses by 10 percent in our area. I therefore need your cooperation in brainstorming on how we can achieve this target."

According to research conducted by organizational psychologist Gary Yukl, actions intended to establish the legitimacy of a request include the following:

* Providing evidence of prior precedent.
* Showing consistency with organizational policies that are involved in the type of request being made.
* Showing consistency with the duties and responsibilities of the person's position or expected roles.
* Indicating that the request has been endorsed by higher management or the person's boss.[2]

Inspirational Appeal and Emotional Display

Making an inspirational appeal is an important influence tactic. You can sometimes inspire others by displaying feelings at the right time, or by appealing to your teammate's emotions. Sup-

2. Gary Yukl, *Skills for Managers and Leaders: Text, Cases, and Exercises* (Englewood Cliffs, N.J.: Prentice-Hall, 1990), pp. 62–63.

pose you needed assistance in completing a report on ways of enhancing customer satisfaction. You might say with a burst of energy and excitement, "If our team can substantially improve customer satisfaction, we will be known as an outrageously successful team. Imagine having recently joined the company and being part of such a winning effort."

For an emotional appeal to be effective, you must understand the values, motives, and goals of the person you are trying to influence. In the influence attempt in question, you are assuming that the new team member takes pride in being part of a winning team. At other times you might make an emotional appeal based on the job insecurity of your influence target. For example, you might suggest that by following your plans, the success the person will achieve could solidify his or her job.

An inspirational appeal will be more effective if you display emotion. Indicators of emotion include talking about feelings, raising and lowering voice tone, showing moist eyes or a few tears, and pounding a table. Talking about feelings include such statements as:

"It would make me happy if you could help me on this project."
"I feel psyched being part of a team that will finally achieve a breakthrough in customer satisfaction."
"I was frightened and apprehensive before I learned that I could enlist a few teammates to help me with this project."
"I get excited when I think of the possibilities of our proposal being approved."

Consultation

Consulting with others before making a decision is an effective influence tactic. The person you are attempting to influence becomes more motivated to follow your request, because he or she is involved in contributing to the decision. In attempting to influence another person by using consultation, you might ask for input while preparing your proposal. An engineer who wanted the support of teammates on a design change she was preparing might consult with them long before her design change was complete.

You are more likely to achieve success with consultation when the objectives of the person being influenced are consistent with yours. In the example at hand, if the influence target also thinks design changes are necessary on the product he or she will be more readily influenced.

Forming a Coalition

At times it is difficult to influence teammates or the team leader by acting alone. An effective technique in these situations is to form coalitions or alliances with others who you know favor your position. Coalitions in business are a numbers game—the more people you can get on your side the better.

A member of a process redesign team wanted to change to a different technique of reengineering because the current one was not producing high-power results. He first obtained the support of his two closest buddies on the team. With three people instead of one supporting this change, he had more clout in convincing several other members. With six people now supporting his position, it was easy to convince the team leader about switching to another reengineering method.

The accompanying list summarizes influence tactics you can use to help you become a breakthrough team player. Using such tactics effectively will reinforce the notion that you are an influential, well-respected member of the team.

Directly Influencing Teammates

1. Rational persuasion
2. Exchanging favors and striking a bargain
3. Legitimizing a request
4. Inspirational appeal and emotional display
5. Consultation
6. Forming a coalition

Now that you have carefully thought through using politics and influence, you can apply some of these skills to the nuts and bolts of team play: performing well in a meeting.

7

Looking Good
at Meetings

Whether you love them or hate them, meetings are the show-place for the breakthrough team player. Even if you accomplish your most significant work by yourself, your teamwork skills are best displayed in a meeting. During a meeting others judge your problem-solving ability, communications effectiveness, leadership ability, and team player attributes. If your goal is to be a breakthrough team player, you have to look good at meetings.

The purpose of this chapter is not to review every sensible suggestion ever made about conducting a meeting, such as preparing an agenda, starting on time, or putting the lid on garrulous participants. Instead, the intent here is to focus on ways of conducting yourself in a meeting that will give you the edge over teammates who rely only on common sense and intuition. Successfully carrying out the leadership roles described in Chapter 4 will also strengthen your contribution as a meeting participant.

The suggestions here are for the team-meeting participants, yet most of the ideas also apply if you are conducting the meeting. In a team-based workplace the distinction between leading and participating in a meeting is blurred. Participants share many of the leadership functions such as note taking, summarizing, and introducing agenda items. Also, participants are often given the opportunity to lead a portion of the meeting focused on their area of expertise.

The information for looking good at meetings is placed in two categories. Category one is information about dealing with the people aspects of meetings. Category two is suggestions for dealing with those aspects of a meeting relating to the task and work processes. The accompanying self-quiz gives you an opportunity to rate your current effectiveness as a meeting participant and pinpoint areas for improvement.

Measuring Your Meeting Effectiveness

Directions: Circle the most accurate number to represent your behavior for each of the following pairs of opposite statements.

My actions and thoughts during a team or group meeting usually:

Increase my credibility	7	6	5	4	3	2	1	Decrease my credibility
Make me look professional	7	6	5	4	3	2	1	Make me look unprofessional
Enhance my leadership image	7	6	5	4	3	2	1	Detract from my leadership image
Make others wish I had stayed home	1	2	3	4	5	6	7	Make others happy I attended the meeting
Encourage others to interact with me	7	6	5	4	3	2	1	Discourage others from interacting with me
Make me look like a solo player	1	2	3	4	5	6	7	Make me look like a team player
Make me appear committed to group goals	7	6	5	4	3	2	1	Make me appear committed to personal goals
Fail to get the results I want	1	2	3	4	5	6	7	Get the results I want
Work for my best interests	7	6	5	4	3	2	1	Work against my best interests
Make me appear disloyal	1	2	3	4	5	6	7	Make me appear loyal

| Make me proud | 7 | 6 | 5 | 4 | 3 | 2 | 1 | Make me feel bad about myself |
| Make me look dis-interested | 1 | 2 | 3 | 4 | 5 | 6 | 7 | Make me look in-terested |

Total score _____

Scoring and interpretation: Find your total by adding the numbers you circled.

72–84   You are quite pleased with your performance and the impression that you create in meetings. Your self-report is that of a breakthrough team player. Watch out for smugness. Find out from others if the highly positive picture you paint is accurate.

50–71   You see your performance in meetings as a mixture of positive and negative aspects. Your candor is to be admired. Read on to obtain some additional ideas for looking good at meetings, and therefore taking an important step toward becoming a breakthrough team player.

12–49   At your own admission, your actions and thoughts during a meeting require considerable improvement. You dislike meetings, and you will have to become more tolerant to become a breakthrough team player.

Dealing With the Human Aspects of Meetings

The major purpose of conducting a team meeting is to deal with a task issue such as improving quality, productivity, or a work process. The team gets together to share information or solve problems related to these major agenda. To accomplish tasks on the agenda, the leader and team members have to work with each other. The way in which you deal with people during a meeting profoundly shapes how you are perceived by them. Your technical contribution might be devalued if you are perceived by others as having poor interpersonal skills.

The focus here is on the more subtle aspects of creating a

favorable impression during a team meeting. Use the information as a reminder of what to do and not do to help you achieve breakthrough status as a team player.

Time Your Contributions

Assume that you have a breakthrough idea you want to contribute during a team meeting. *When* you introduce your suggestion can have a major impact on its acceptance. Observe sharply when the group seems receptive to hearing an important contribution. During the warm-up phase of the meeting, team members may not be mentally prepared to listen carefully to an important suggestion. If you wait until the team has processed several major agenda items, they might not be interested in weighing the pros and cons of another suggestion. A generally effective tactic is to introduce your idea shortly after the warm-up banter has been completed.

Another aspect of timing is to wait for a lull in the action. Your teammates will be more receptive to dealing with a potentially breakthrough item if they are not in the midst of processing another idea.

Many a good idea has fallen flat because of physiological interference. If people are preoccupied with thoughts of a food and beverage break or a rest room break, they will not be receptive to a new idea that will postpone the break. Afterwards, team members can again concentrate on higher-level concerns.

Effective timing also means offering your breakthrough idea when most of the team is in a good mood. When most of the team is angry, irritated, or stressed out for other reasons, members may not be mentally prepared to think positively.

Avoid Leaving the Meeting, Except for Emergencies

Being physically present or absent from a meeting would appear to be a task issue, because you cannot work on agenda items with the team unless you are physically present. A people issue is also involved because the act of leaving the meeting connotes that you have more pressing matters on your mind than attending the meeting. Leaving and returning several times during the meeting can create a worse impression than leaving just once. Leaving once and not returning could suggest that you have an all-consuming problem to handle. Leaving and returning several times to the meeting creates the impression that you are willing to give only minimum compliance to the meeting.

A particularly offensive attitude is to imply that if a high-ranking organizational official wants to see you, it is perfectly understandable to leave the meeting. People who leave immediately when signaled by a high-ranking manager typically expect teammates to accept the legitimacy of their exit. Often they say in a whisper, "The *vice president* asked to see me." Teammates feel slighted because they are expected to assume that a meeting with the vice president is unquestionably more important than spending time in their meeting.

Leaving a team meeting suddenly to comply with a high-ranking manager's request creates ill will for another reason. In a team-based organization, the team is supposed to have high status. Correspondingly, hierarchical rank is supposed to be less important. By assuming that meeting with a high-ranking person is more important than your obligations to the team at the moment, you are thinking traditionally about power and authority in organizations. (You may be right, but people in a team-based culture prefer to think idealistically.)

Be Supportive of Other Members

Being supportive is so important that it is a recognized team member role. If another participant in a team meeting says something of value, give that person your approval by such means as nodding or smiling. Support of this type encourages the free flow of ideas. Supportiveness includes tolerance for viewpoints considerably different from yours. Supportiveness increases your stature in the team because it projects an impression of concern for the welfare of others. Team members are favorably disposed toward other members who support them and will often be prepared to return the favor.

Show by Your Nonverbal and Verbal Behavior That You Are Listening

Every reader of this book knows that an effective team member listens carefully to team members. Listening is expected, and therefore hardly praiseworthy. To ensure that you do not lose points for appearing to be an ineffective listener, remember to engage in such nonverbal behaviors as:

* Nodding with either approval or disapproval.
* Taking notes after the person has finished a major point.
* Leaning toward the person and maintaining eye contact while he or she is presenting.
* Rocking back and forth in your chair with your arms crossed and your tongue planted in a cheek. (Practice this one in front of a mirror or video camera a few times before implementation.)
* Looking attentive by opening your eyes widely and frowning occasionally. If you feel compelled to yawn, close your mouth while yawning. (The close-mouthed yawn takes practice. Consult a veteran of hundreds of meetings.)

Supplement your nonverbal behavior with verbal indicators of listening. These include asking a question after a person completes a point, and offering a one- or two-line summary. Assume that a teammate has made a five-minute presentation on the importance of conducting research about customer preferences. You respond, "Your point is that we should talk to our customers?"

Respond to the Comments of Other Participants

Interacting with teammates is important because it has a brainstorming effect—new ideas build on the ideas of others. If you react frequently to the ideas of others, particularly in a positive way, you will be perceived by some team members as a spark plug. Igniting the ideas of others is an important contribution to the team effort and will therefore enhance your stature as a key player on the team.

Responding critically to the comments of teammates can also make a contribution to team functioning, and make you look good in the process. A tactful challenge is sometimes in order. You might confront another team member about a digression with a statement such as, "I, too, am concerned about our country's rising trade deficit with Pacific Rim countries, but let's deal with our company's diversity initiative."

Serve as a Role Model for Others

Whether a team leader or a team member, you can help set the tone for the meeting. If you are insistent, domineering, or overly quick to criticize others you could be encouraging others to behave similarly. In contrast, if you are calm, reasonable, and reflective, then others—within the limits of their personality—will tend to behave similarly.

Encourage Candid Comments

A dull, ceremonial meeting is characterized by participants offering only polite, psychologically safe comments. In contrast, an exciting, results-oriented meeting is characterized by members contributing candid comments about agenda items and related topics. If you do your bit to accept criticism from teammates, you will be helping to raise the level of candor.

Suppose a teammate says, "What good does it do for us to sit here and dream up ways to improve quality? Top management has such low regard for employee welfare that they will not be motivated to do quality work." To encourage this type of candor without turning the meeting into a gripe session, you might respond, "That's an interesting comment. What suggestions could we as a team make to help top management be more concerned about employee welfare?" By making such a comment you are sharing leadership responsibility with the team leader.

Be Tolerant of Divergent Views

Encouraging candor relates closely to creating an atmosphere that tolerates diverse viewpoints and controversial opinions. Toleration can be communicated by subtle behavior such as a nod of approval or a wink after another participant has expressed an extreme viewpoint. The nod, wink, or similar behavior does not necessarily imply agreement, but it does imply acceptance of divergent views.

A team took on the small project of planning a year-end party. Katrina, an iconoclastic team member, suggested that perhaps the team should think outside the box. In her mind, the team's real purpose was to provide a morale-building experience for employees. She said, "Why the same-old paradigm of a year-end party? Most employees' schedules are overloaded with parties at year-end. Maybe a lot of people would like to have a holiday party in February when parties are scarce.

"Besides, maybe most employees don't want a company-sponsored party. What would happen if we gave employees a choice between a party and $50 in cash—roughly the cost of an employee and a spouse or friend to attend the party?"

Several team members scoffed at Katrina's suggestions, but Raoul did not. He encouraged Katrina to continue with her analysis and then suggested that the team investigate the validity of her claims. Katrina's research showed that a year-end party was preferred by only a 10 percent margin. Raoul showed breakthrough qualities by his tolerance for thinking outside the box.

Act as a Mediator

A high-level skill for the team player or team leader is to act as a mediator to resolve disputes within the group. Being able to mediate disputes will enhance your reputation as a major contributor to the group effort. When divergent views are encouraged, differences of opinion on important issues will surface frequently. The stage is thus set for mediation.

During a meeting, several members might support an important proposal, while others might be opposed. Suppose a proposal for converting entirely to a voice-mail system is being countered by one to retain some office assistants to answer phones. You might introduce the idea of taking a large sheet of paper with a line down the middle. The pros and cons of switching or not switching entirely to voice mail can then be listed. All team members are asked to participate.

Each of the arguments can be discussed briefly. Such a procedure enables all participants to hear clearly the positive and negative aspects of the conflicting proposals before taking a final stand.[1] If the issue is resolved satisfactorily, you will be recognized as an effective mediator. Should the issue not be resolved completely, you will still receive credit for having introduced a useful technique for resolving future differences of opinion. The accompanying list will serve as a quick review of the points about looking good in a meeting by dealing with its human aspects.

Dealing With the Human Aspects of Meetings

1. Time your contributions.
2. Avoid leaving the meeting, except for emergencies.
3. Be supportive of other members.
4. Show by nonverbal and verbal behavior that you are listening.
5. Respond to the comments of other participants.
6. Serve as a role model for others.
7. Encourage candid comments.
8. Be tolerant of divergent views.
9. Act as a mediator.

Dealing With the Task Aspects of Meetings

The task aspects of meetings—including the mechanics of conducting a meeting—provide ample opportunity for the potential breakthrough team player to display his or her mettle. The choice is not between dealing well with people versus dealing well with tasks. Instead, the breakthrough team player has to

1. "Don't Let Discord Ruin Your Meetings," *Personal Report for the Executive* (December 15, 1989), p. 3.

accomplish both. Here are ways a person can impress the team leader and team members by dealing effectively with various aspects of goal attainment.

Make the Optimal Number of Contributions

A breakthrough team player uses intuition to determine the right frequency of contribution to group discussion. One of the most destructive forces on a team can be the participant who is trying harder than everybody else. The person who hogs a meeting is perceived just as negatively as the noncontributor. Carmen, a manufacturing engineer, was assigned to a cross-functional, new ventures team. He explains how one aspect of serving on the team disturbed him:

> Ed, one of the team members, created problems for me. No doubt he had more brainpower than anyone else on the team. His background in finance enabled him to contribute valuable input. But Ed must have used up one-third of the meeting time presenting his point of view. What he had to contribute was usually valuable, so the team leader didn't want to discourage him entirely.
>
> After a while, it got sickening listening to Ed go on at length explaining his opinion on every issue. He spoke loud, and he spoke often. After the first four months of serving on the team, I felt like I was taking a course from Ed. It was an old-fashioned type of course in which the instructor does all the talking and the students do all the listening.

The challenge in determining the right number of contributions is to give other people a chance but not be so polite that you appear passive. As a rule of thumb, think toward making one good contribution per hour of meeting. When you are not contributing ideas, it doesn't mean you are inactive. You will still be encouraging others, giving support, and perhaps taking a few notes. Contributions (not just any comment) at the rate of one per hour will keep you in the limelight without people getting tired of hearing from you.

How frequently you contribute will also be shaped by the nature of the meeting. At times your unique expertise will call for more contributions on your part. Even in these circumstances, however, be sensitive to avoid dominating the meeting. Ask someone else to contribute who has related expertise, or who is familiar with part of the ideas you are contributing.

Keep Your Comments Brief and to the Point

After you have decided on the optimum number of contributions, you should still monitor the length of your contribution. In a fast-paced, high-action meeting, most contributions should be brief and to the point. Focus sharply on the problem at hand. Aside from lowering the productivity of meetings, irrelevant comments annoy other members. If your point requires lengthy explanation and documentation, inform your teammates that within twenty-four hours you will supply them with an e-mail or hard-copy presentation of the details. Such a maneuver is bound to impress, so long as the information you send along is valuable.

Help the Team Stick to the Agenda

Despite everybody knowing that an agenda is important, team meetings often slip away from following the agenda. Staying on track is the most frequently violated principle of conducting a productive meeting. Helping your teammates follow the agenda contributes to your being perceived as a key member of the team. Here are two agenda-sticking and agenda-returning tactics you can use during a meeting:

1. Look down at your watch, then look up. Say to the group, "Look gang, it's 11:30 now. We've been at this since 8:30 this morning. So far we've processed [*great buzzword*] only one agenda item. Shouldn't we be moving faster?"
2. You pick up your pencil, and say to the team, "I've done

a quick little analysis here. During the last twenty minutes, we've only had three minutes of discussion related directly to the agenda. Are we taking our agenda seriously enough?"

Encourage the Team to Use a Systematic Problem-Solving Method

As knowledge of how to conduct meetings has become more widespread, a higher proportion of meetings are productive. Nevertheless, many problem-solving meetings fail to meet their intended purpose. Instead of a problem being solved, tangents are pursued with diligence. Furthermore, many meetings are working on the wrong problem. An example of working on the wrong problem would be looking for ways to cut costs, when the real problem is how to motivate workers to be cost-conscious.

One way to enhance the productivity of meetings is to use a systematic problem-solving method. Systematic approaches to problem-solving are based on the scientific method, and are therefore similar to one another. If you encourage the team to use an orderly group-decision-making process, your status will be enhanced. Your team is likely to have more productive meetings if you adhere closely to the steps for effective group decision making, as described next. You will be remembered for having introduced this well-established process.

1. *Identify the problem.* Describe specifically what the problem is and how it manifests itself. If your true problem is not identified, you will never find a true solution.
2. *Clarify your problem.* If team members do not perceive the problem the same way, they will offer possibly divergent solutions to their individual perceptions of the problem.
3. *Analyze the cause.* To convert "what is" into "what we want," the group must understand the causes of the specific problem and find ways to overcome these causes.
4. *Search for alternative solutions.* Remember that multiple solutions can be found to most problems. To display your breakthrough qualities, be imaginative in generating alternative solutions.

5. *Select alternatives.* Identify the criteria that solutions must meet, then discuss the pros and cons of the proposed alternatives. In the spirit of brainstorming, no solution should be laughed at or scorned.
6. *Plan for implementation.* Decide what actions are necessary to carry out the chosen solution to the problem.
7. *Clarify the contract.* The contract is a statement of what group members have agreed to and deadlines for accomplishment. Many teams lose potential productivity because this step is omitted.
8. *Develop an action plan.* Specify who does what and when to carry out the contract.
9. *Provide for evaluation and accountability.* After the plan is implemented, reconvene to discuss the progress, and hold team members accountable for results that have not been achieved.[2]

If your team accomplishes all of the above nine steps, you will be part of a breakthrough team inspired by a breakthrough team player. If you do not get to all of the steps, at least use some of them. Teams are sometimes successful in using the above model even though they do not follow the steps in precise order.

Influence Others to Use High Technology to Facilitate the Meeting

Advances in telecommunications can facilitate meetings. As a team leader or team member, take the initiative to introduce some aspects of this high technology into your team meetings. Four important new advances are laptop computers, electronic meetings, software for planning meetings, and video-conferencing. If any of these new developments become part of team operations and they work well, you will be remembered for your contribution.

2. List based on Andrew E. Schwartz and Joy Levin, "Better Group Decision Making," *Supervisory Magazine* (June 1990), p. 4.

• Depending on how you use one, a laptop computer can enhance or detract from your team player status. On the positive side, taking notes during the meeting with a laptop makes you appear modern and can enhance the quality of the notes. The laptop can also be the basis for feeding information on to a large monitor or movie screen to display graphics. All highly impressive.

A distinct disadvantage of using a laptop during a team meeting is that you can get so caught up in working the keyboard that you rarely look at teammates or contribute ideas. The note-taker with the laptop slips into the role of a court reporter: faithfully recording information but detached from the meeting.

• Electronic meetings allow participants to work on the same problem simultaneously by using a linked set of computers. The problem appears on each team member's computer monitor. Participants can suggest a solution to the problem by entering it into the computer. These solutions are displayed to all the other members. Participants can modify each other's solutions. The monitors display the revised problem solutions, allowing participants to see others' solutions simultaneously. The system is particularly well suited for "what if" discussions. At the end of the meeting, all participants receive a printout of the results.

A behavioral advantage of an electronic meeting is that shy people are not dominated by forceful personalities. Each participant has an equal opportunity to submit ideas—providing the person has adequate keyboard and computer graphics skills. If you and/or other participants are struggling with the technology, operating the system takes precedence over creative thought.

• Software for planning meetings helps organize them in ways similar to the suggestions made in this and the previous section. An example is The Facilitator, which allows the user to tell the program the objective of the meeting, the location, and the starting time. Another window allows the leader or team members to enter the agenda and the amount of time to be spent on each agenda item. At the meeting, an alarm in the program indicates when it is time to move on to the next agenda item. As ideas are generated in the meeting, they are entered into the computer and categorized into buckets or categories. The Facilitator also records who voted for which alternative and prints the minutes at the conclusion of the meeting.

• After a slow start, video-conferencing is gaining acceptance as a way to reduce travel costs associated with gathering people for a meeting. Given that the vast majority of teams are composed of people from the same work site, video-conferencing has limited applicability for teamwork with one important exception. The virtual corporation (networks of companies sharing resources) relies on a team of people working together from remote locations. If you are a member of a virtual corporation, you might suggest the use of video-conferencing to supplement face-to-face get-togethers.

At a video conference, people in different locations can talk to each other while viewing each other's image on a television screen. In addition to reducing travel costs, video conferences can increase productivity because participants only have to travel to a video-conferencing center near their office. A video conference, however, may create some communication problems because it still lacks the give and take of in-person interactions. Some nonverbal communication is lost because the conference members act more stiffly than in person.

You need an outstanding video personality to be a breakthrough team player at a video conference. If you decide to recommend video-conferencing or if your company is already using the technology, practice making presentations in front of a camcorder.

Conclude on a Positive Note

A magnificently simple way of using task issues to show breakthrough qualities is to end your meeting on a positive note. The meeting leader is ordinarily in the best position to make the concluding statement, but any member can make a positive comment close to the end of the meeting.

Team members should leave the meeting with a feeling of having accomplished something worthwhile. If there has been much disagreement and not much visible progress, the leader or an assertive team member should point out what went right in the meeting. For example, you might say, "My impression is that we did not agree on goals for the quarter, but we did agree that we should set them."

The following list outlines key points for dealing effectively with the task aspects of meetings. Combining these skills with people-oriented skills will enable you to perform exceptionally well at team meetings.

Dealing With the Task Aspect of Meetings

1. Make the optimal number of contributions.
2. Keep your comments brief and to the point.
3. Help the team stick to the agenda.
4. Encourage the team to use a systematic problem-solving method.
5. Influence others to use high technology to facilitate the meeting.
6. Conclude on a positive note.

Our book so far has focused on you as a team player, often exercising leadership without holding a formal leadership position. The next two chapters focus on your role as a team leader.

8

The People Side of Team Leadership

An extension of being a breakthrough team player is to be an effective team leader. If you have been an outstanding team player, you will most likely have one or more opportunities to hold a formal team leadership assignment. You might be appointed to a long-term leadership position such as project manager. Another possibility is that you could be given a series of short-term team leadership assignments, including the head of a task force. As a formal leader, you will still need to practice your teamwork skills. A team leader is also a player on his or her team.

The purpose of this chapter is to highlight key attitudes, skills, and practices that relate to the people side of effective team leadership. In the following chapter, the focus is on the task side of team leadership. Take the accompanying quiz to evaluate how well your attitudes and practices fit the demands of the people side of team leadership.

The Team Leadership Attitudes Quiz

Directions: Respond to the following statements as they relate to your leadership experience. If you do not have leadership experience, on or off the job, imagine how you would act or think if you were a team leader. Indicate the extent to which you agree or disagree with each of the following statements: strongly agree (SA); agree (A); neutral (N); disagree (D);

strongly disagree (SD). Circle the number under the most accurate answer for each question.

	SA	A	N	D	SD
1. I prefer to make important decisions myself without consulting team members.	1	2	3	4	5
2. I am willing to confront team members with mistakes they have made.	5	4	3	2	1
3. Good work is its own reward. Team members therefore do not need frequent praise from the leader.	1	2	3	4	5
4. New team members should work hard for a long time before they are fully accepted as a team member.	1	2	3	4	5
5. A person is likely to be effective as a team leader when using a command-and-control style of leadership.	1	2	3	4	5
6. A person is likely to be effective as a team leader when using a coaching style of leadership.	5	4	3	2	1
7. A little intimidation can go a long way in developing a winning team.	1	2	3	4	5
8. I compete intensely against other managers and team leaders in my organization.	1	2	3	4	5
9. Team members with a professional attitude require very little praise and encouragement from the team leader.	1	2	3	4	5
10. An effective way of motivating a team is to create an "in group" and an "out group."	1	2	3	4	5
11. I give frequent feedback to both high performers and low performers.	5	4	3	2	1

	SA	A	N	D	SD
12. Part of a team leader's time should be spent in developing a vision for the team.	5	4	3	2	1
13. As a team leader, I like to keep tight control over as many details as possible.	1	2	3	4	5
14. To enhance communication effectiveness I attempt to discourage the use of in-group jargon.	1	2	3	4	5
15. A major part of my job as a team leader is to serve the team members.	5	4	3	2	1

Total score _____

Scoring and interpretation: Add up the numbers you have circled, and use the following guide to evaluate the fitness of your attitudes for effectively handling the people side of team leadership.

65–75   You have an up-to-date and highly effective set of attitudes about dealing with the human aspects of team leadership. Read ahead with enjoyment to build on the fine sensitivity to team leadership you already possess.

31–64   Your attitudes reflect an average suitability for dealing with the human aspects of team leadership. You would profit from sharpening your insights into the interpersonal aspects of leadership.

15–30   Your current attitudes about the human aspects of team leadership may not be a good fit for a team-based organizational culture. Study this chapter, along with one or two current leadership books, carefully.

The information presented here about the people-oriented side of team leadership is organized into three sections: two effective leadership styles; establishing a teamwork culture, and fostering team spirit.

Two Effective Team Leadership Styles

Widespread agreement exists that the preferred leadership style in a team-based organization is for the leader to act as a facilitator instead of an autocrat. Rather than tell people what to do, the effective team leader helps bring out the best among team members. Team leaders make their mark by serving the best interests of team members. In the process, they help the organization. Two related leadership styles in particular propel the team leader toward being a facilitator: the coaching style and the servant leader.

The Coaching Leadership Style

The team structure elevates the importance of coaching. As a coach, the team leader makes on-the-spot suggestions for performance and offers team members frequent encouragement. The coach also blows the whistle when a team member makes a bad move—such as an ethical violation—and offers suggestions for improvement. Coaching is also important because it adds a human touch to a competitive, seemingly unfeeling workplace.

To be a breakthrough team leader, you have to coach team members frequently. Here we look at the most important actions associated with the coaching style of team leadership.

1. *Provide specific feedback.* To coach a team member toward higher levels of performance, pinpoint what behavior, attitude, or skill requires improvement. An effective team coach might say, "I read your proposal for forming true partnerships without suppliers. It's acceptable but it falls short of your usual level of creativity. You haven't specified any new actions we should take in dealing with suppliers. Have you thought about . . . ?"

2. *Provide ample positive reinforcement.* A key part of a coach's job is to give positive reinforcement when a team member does something right. Just the act of giving positive feedback is rewarding. Successful team leaders also give deserving members recognition, praise, and other rewards such as an opportunity to take on a high-status, challenging assignment.

3. *Be an active listener.* As an active listener, attempt to grasp both the facts and feelings of what is said. Observing the team member's nonverbal communication is another part of active listening. Be patient and do not be poised for a rebuttal to any difference of opinion between you and a team member.

4. *Give emotional support.* Giving emotional support is the linchpin of a team leader's job. By being helpful and constructive, the team leader provides much-needed emotional support to the team member who is not performing at his or her best. An effective way of giving emotional support is to use positive rather than negative motivators. For example, as the team leader you might say, "I liked some things you did yesterday. Yet I have a few suggestions that might bring you closer to peak performance."

Another way to give emotional support is to express sympathy and understanding when a team member is stressed out. Use a comment such as, "I recognize you've been doing the work of one and one-half people lately. We need your contribution, and it is much appreciated."

5. *Reflect feelings.* An effective team leader is adept at reflecting feelings. Reflection-of-feeling responses typically begin with "You feel. . . ." The team member might say, "I've never been so overloaded in the ten years I've worked here." The team leader responds, "You feel that the workload is excessive." Now feeling understood, the team member would start pouring out concerns about being so overworked. The full expression of feelings would set the stage for formulating constructive action plans to deal with the problem.

6. *Give constructive advice.* Too much advice-giving interferes with two-way communication, yet some advice can elevate performance. The team leader should assist the team member to answer the question, "What can I do about this problem?" Advice in the form of a question or suppositional statement is often effective.

7. *Be a model of what you expect.* An effective team leader shows others by example the kind of behavior he or she thinks is desirable. For instance, the team leader should be visibly cooperative with people from other organizational units if he or

she wants team members to cooperate with each other. The breakthrough team leader avoids comments such as, "Those _____ from finance want to analyze our spending pattern. They're so paranoid, they trust nobody."

8. *Gain a commitment to change.* Unless the team leader receives a commitment from the team member to carry through with the proposed solution to a problem, the team member may not improve performance. An experienced team leader/coach develops an intuitive feel for when team members are serious about performance improvement. One clue that commitment to change is lacking is agreeing without any hesitation about the need for change. Another is agreeing to change without display of emotion.

The Servant Leader

Another style that fits the philosophy of team leadership is to be a *servant leader.* A team leader in the new workplace is required to devote less energy to pleasing the boss and more energy to helping the team succeed. According to the idea of servant leadership, strong leadership is provided when the person at the helm is concerned about taking care of group members. The team leader also asks team members what needs to be done.[1]

By definition, the servant leader works to support the best interests of team members. The leader makes sure that the team is getting an equitable share of resources and rewards. A servant team leader will approach the next level of management as an advocate for the group, as illustrated by the actions of a team leader at an electronics components company:

Jan was the team leader for a small group that manufactured the on-screen menus for television sets. The menus enabled the person operating the television set to select such options as closed captioning, automatic programming, and choosing among three languages for reading the menu. Because the demand for this product had

1. Robert M. Tomasko, *Rethinking the Corporation: The Architecture of Change* (New York: AMACOM, 1993), pp. 160–161.

surged so dramatically, Jan's team could hardly keep up with it.

As Jan's team planned to add three more computer technicians to the team, the company announced a hiring freeze. Instead of accepting the freeze without question, Jan brought her case to upper management. She demonstrated how hiring three more manufacturing technicians would be highly cost effective for the company. Jan made three different presentations to management pleading the case for her team.

Top management accepted her logic, and the team was able to hire the three computer technicians it needed to keep up with demand.

A team leader who acts as a servant leader helps keep the group focused on serving customers and building products or services, instead of preparing information for higher management. The team leader takes care of requests from the executive suite. He or she might even challenge upper management as to why certain information is needed.

Management consultant Robert M. Tomasko illustrates servant leadership in practice. If you ask a FedEx employee how many group members report to his or her manager, the employee will probably say something like, "Sorry, you seem to have it backwards. My manager works for the twelve of us to help us succeed at our jobs."[2]

The two effective leadership styles presented here are not mutually exclusive. A breakthrough team leader can blend the two, depending on the needs of the occasion. An effective coach, for example, can also be a servant leader when the team needs help in its dealings outside the team.

Establishing a Teamwork Culture

A major challenge relating to the people side of team leadership is to establish a culture that fosters teamwork. Although top

2. Ibid., p. 161.

management has the lion's share of the responsibility for establishing an organizational culture, the team leader also contributes to the development of culture. He or she can contribute to
a subculture that fosters teamwork.

The strategy for the breakthrough team leader is to promote
the attitude that working together effectively is an expected
standard of conduct. Developing a culture (or norm) of teamwork will be difficult when a strong culture of individualism
exists within the larger company. Yet the leader can otherwise
make progress toward establishing a teamwork norm. Specific
tactics to support the strategy of fostering a teamwork culture
are described next.

Encourage Team Members to Treat Each Other as If They Were External Customers

According to members of the total quality movement, everybody
with whom you interact is your customer. Nevertheless, most
workers treat external customers with more respect and concern
than they do company employees at or below their level. Some
team leaders encourage team members to treat each other as if
they were external customers, thus fostering cooperative behavior and politeness. Treating team members as external customers
would involve such actions as:

- Taking a team member to lunch just to maintain a working relationship
- Asking a teammate if you could help her solve a difficult
  problem
- Asking a teammate exactly the kind of input he needed
  so you could do an outstanding job of helping him

Treating teammates as external customers would also involve concern about holding on to good working relationships
with them. One team member would therefore worry if another
team member did not consult with her for a long time.

Get People to Trust Each Other and Upper Management

Mutual trust is a bedrock condition for high levels of teamwork and cooperation. If team members do not trust each other, they will hold back on full mutual cooperation. Not trusting upper management is also a deterrent to high levels of teamwork. Getting team members to trust each other is more under your control than getting them to trust upper management. The reason is that the team leader exerts a more direct influence over interactions within the group than he or she does over top management policies and practices.

One way of enhancing mutual trust is to encourage team members to give honest feedback to each other during team meetings. For example, one team member might say to another, "I would be more eager to join your subcommittee if you took deadlines more seriously." Holding candid meetings can also engender trust. Candor leads to trust because openly expressing one's opinion leads others to think the person tends not to hide opinions and information. Another trust builder is for team members to fully disclose the type of work they are performing outside of shared team activities.

Distrust of top management often comes about when team members perceive that their best efforts are not rewarded or even backfire. In the heyday of quality circles, many members of the circle teams became discouraged because their suggestions were ignored so frequently. Team efforts backfire also if the productivity increases of the team result in the need for fewer workers and subsequent layoffs.

A top-management commitment to avoiding involuntary layoffs as a result of productivity improvements by teams will increase trust in organizational leadership. NYNEX, a telecommunications company in the northeastern United States, took such action to bolster sagging morale during layoffs. The company reached the painful decision in the early 1990s that it had to eliminate the jobs of 17,000 workers, almost one-third of its workforce. In place of large-scale layoffs, NYNEX and the Communications Workers of America agreed to a new contract that all but guaranteed no involuntary layoffs.

Get the Team to Spend Time Together

A team becomes more cohesive as a function of spending more time together. Team meetings are obviously important, as are group breakfasts, luncheons, and after-hours parties. Team leaders have to be careful, however, not to exacerbate the ever expanding workweek for professionals. As a valuation specialist on a mergers and acquisition team said, "A Friday evening drink together with the team is yet another meeting on my cramped schedule. It's one more early evening away from the family." In addition to working together face-to-face, e-mail and telephone interactions also help build teamwork.

Make Frequent Use of Terms and Phrases That Support Teamwork

A team is designed to be a democratic structure in which hierarchical rank and other status differences are not so pronounced. Emphasizing the words *team members* or *teammates*, and deemphasizing the words *subordinates* and *employees* helps communicate the norm of teamwork and a teamwork culture.

A divisive distinction to avoid is essential versus nonessential work. For example, a team leader is advised not to say to the group, "Soon we may have to terminate those among us who are doing nonessential work." (In the language of the slash and burn manager, the only *essential* work deals with making and selling products and services, thus excluding about two-thirds of the workforce.)

Earlier in the book, you were advised to make frequent use of the terms *we* and *us*. The same advice applies when you occupy a formal leadership role. Pepper your conversation with phrases such as "our team," "we achieved this," and "we can do it." Frequent use of the term *team* is another direct way of promoting teamwork.

Emphasize the Fact That Yours Is a Winning Team

Teams with the best records of accomplishment have the best teamwork. Conversely, teams with the best teamwork have the best records of accomplishment. Whether winning teams create good teamwork or the reverse, it pays to emphasize that yours is a winning team. Remind team members frequently of what your team is doing that is above average, and consequently why they belong to a winning team.

Most teams are particularly good at some task. The leader should help the group identify that task and promote it as a key strength. A shipping department, for example, might have the best on-time shipping record in the region. Or a claims processing unit might have the fewest overpayments in an insurance company.

T. J. Rodgers, the CEO of Cypress Semiconductors, involves himself in the recruitment of managers and professionals throughout the company. The recruiting lure he emphasizes is the opportunity to join a winning team. Rodgers says that for many candidates, the opportunity to join a winner is more important than finding the highest paying job. He also observes that recruiting people who want to be winners results in a company with better teamwork.[3]

The accompanying list summarizes the points made about establishing a teamwork culture. Each item can serve as a reminder of action steps the leader can take when trying to meld a group of individuals into a team.

Establishing a Teamwork Culture

1. Encourage team members to treat each other as if they were external customers.
2. Get people to trust each other and upper management.
3. Get the team to spend time together.
4. Make frequent use of terms and phrases that support teamwork.
5. Emphasize the fact that yours is a winning team.

3. T. J. Rodgers, "Scouting for Talent: A Surefire Plan to Capture and Keep Top Performers," *Success* (December 1993), p. 80.

Fostering Team Spirit

Closely associated with establishing a teamwork culture is for the leader to engage in actions and express attitudes that foster a team spirit. Without esprit de corps, the potential advantages of team structures cannot be realized. With high team spirit, a group of individuals can achieve synergy.

Promote a Vision and a Mission

Top executives set a vision for the company, yet teams can have their own visions that support the vision at the top. The leader of a product development team might encourage the team to establish a vision of someday becoming a world-class product development group. Given that most corporate visions are lofty, team visions will usually fit a corporate vision relating to world-class status.

A mission is typically more specific than a vision and tied more directly to the team's present reality, such as "providing outstanding products for the company to manufacture." Whether you spur the team to establish a vision, mission, or both it will be an important step forward in developing teamwork.

Build Commitment and Confidence

Jon R. Katzenbach and Douglas K. Smith urge the team leader to build the commitment and confidence of each team member as well as that of the team as a whole. For the group to develop a strong team spirit, individuals must feel a sense of mutual accountability. An effective vehicle for building commitment and confidence is to make ample use of positive reinforcement.[4] Team members should be given frequent reminders of what they are doing right and encouraged for actions they take that contribute to team goals. A store manager at Wegman's, the largest

---

4. Jon R. Katzenbach and Douglas K. Smith, *The Wisdom Teams: Creating the High-Performance Organization* (New York: Harper Business, 1993), p. 193.

independent supermarket chain in the United States, describes her approach to building commitment and confidence:

> The majority of our store associates are part-time workers, so it's not too easy to build commitment. Yet it can be done. When we have had an outstanding day for sales, such as the day before the Super Bowl, I let every associate know how great the team did. Store associates who receive compliments from customers have their names placed on the wall. We try not to let anybody's contribution go unnoticed. I think we have an outstanding team in my store. Our turnover is below average and our sales are extraordinary.

It cannot be stated with much certainty that positive reinforcement leads directly to commitment and confidence, and builds team spirit. What can be stated is that giving people no positive reinforcement decreases commitment and confidence, and lowers team spirit.

Emphasize Group Recognition

Giving rewards for group accomplishment reinforces teamwork, because people receive rewards for what they have achieved collaboratively. The recognition accompanying the reward should emphasize the team's value to the organization rather than to the individual. Recognition promotes team spirit by enabling the team to take pride in its contributions and progress. Three examples of team recognition follow:

1. A display wall for postings related to team activities, such as certificates of accomplishment, schedules, and miscellaneous announcements
2. Team logos on items, such as identifying T-shirts, athletic caps, mugs, jackets, key rings, and business cards
3. Celebrations to mark milestones, such as first-time activities, cost savings, and safety records

Instill Team Spirit by Welcoming All Input

Team spirit increases with a broad-based contribution to the team effort. It is especially important for the breakthrough team leader to avoid the situation of one or two people on the team being carried by the other contributors. Unfortunately, not every member of the team has the talent to contribute as much as the stronger members. Welcome all input to encourage even modest contributions. Explain how each idea, each completed task, contributes to the larger fabric of the team product.

A team meeting was devoted to designing a configuration for a home entertainment center. Marca, the newest member of the product development team, had a perplexed look. Sanford, the team leader, smiled at Marca and asked her why she looked perplexed. Marca replied that she was concerned because she had no breakaway suggestion to make. Sanford reassured her that sometimes a very small suggestion makes the difference in a winning product.

Marca responded, "Okay, then here is my idea. I think you should equip the cabinet with casters that will move on deep carpeting. Most cabinets containing heavy equipment are a struggle to move around on heavy carpeting." The team cheered, and Marca felt great.

Create Opportunities for Others

If the team leader hogs the best opportunities, assignments, and credits, it will dampen team spirit and team performance. One of a leader's biggest challenges is to provide opportunities for the team and team members to perform well. The challenge is more acute when the team leader is a person with a strong track record, and the other team members are at an earlier career stage.

Top management at an entertainment conglomerate decided to investigate the possibilities of opening a theme park. The head of the new venture team was asked to personally visit six leading theme parks in the United States and Canada. She welcomed the assignment but then suggested to top management, "Jeff, one of the quickest minds on the team, is also a theme park buff. He even wears a Mickey Mouse watch. I recommend we send him on this field assignment. His insights would be very helpful." The executive group welcomed the suggestion. The team knew without the team leader saying so that she had passed a plum assignment along to a team member.

Engage in the Tasks Performed by the Team

One of my earliest work experiences taught me a lesson about team leadership that is still valid today. The first day I showed up to work for my entry-level job at a diner, the manager was busily mopping the floor. I assumed that since I had arrived on the scene, the mop detail would be handed to me. Instead, the manager told me, "Look sonny, I mop the floors just like anybody else. I'd never ask anybody working for me to do a job I wouldn't do."

Breakthrough team leaders have the same team-spirit-building attitude. A team leader performs many of the tasks performed by team members, including analytical work, calling on accounts, and crunching numbers. The idealized version of a leader who spends all his or her time formulating visions, crafting strategic plans, and inspiring others through charisma does not fit team leadership. The team leader engages in some work that is strictly the leader's responsibility, such as arriving at a final decision after listening to group input. Yet much of the team leader's job overlaps with that of team members, at least in groups where team spirit and productivity are high.

Introduce Humor With Appropriate Frequency

Humor and laughter are excellent vehicles for building team spirit when used with appropriate frequency. The group needs to laugh enough to raise morale, to increase the fun associated with the team task, and to stimulate creativity. The breakthrough team leader therefore has a good sense of humor but avoids the immaturity of a nonstop office clown. For building team spirit, the most effective humor is linked to the situation in the form of a humorous comment. Bringing rehearsed jokes into team meetings is much less effective. Here are two examples of humor that worked in specific situations. Recognize that outside of the situational context, a statement may not appear so humorous.

1. A production work team was attempting to fill a position for a CAD/CAM (computer assisted design/computer assisted manufacturing) technician to join the team. A team member said she had an excellent candidate, but that his current salary was $3,500 higher than the maximum starting salary for this position. With a deadpan expression the team leader said, "Call him back and see if he's interested in taking a pay cut."

2. During a troubled period at ITT, a senior financial executive began a meeting by sketching an ocean liner on a flip chart. Next, he printed in large letters, ITT. The other members of the team stared intently and burst into laughter when the executive added six more letters to form ITTitanic.

Encourage the Use of In-Group Jargon

Conventional wisdom is that jargon should be minimized in business. Yet liberal use of jargon among team members enhances team spirit because it sets the team apart from others in the organization. When dealing with outsiders, team members can then follow the principle of minimizing jargon. Teams performing specialized work are the most likely to use jargon. For example, a team member from a quality-improvement team returned from vacation. Asked how his golf game was during vacation, he replied, "Far too much variation to achieve zero defects." (In this situation, jargon was combined with humor.)

Before moving on to the next chapter, which focuses on task aspects of team leadership, review the accompanying list.

Suggestions for Fostering Team Spirit

1. Promote a vision and a mission.
2. Build commitment and confidence.
3. Emphasize group recognition.
4. Instill team spirit by welcoming all input.
5. Create opportunities for others.
6. Engage in the tasks performed by the team.
7. Encourage the use of in-group jargon.
8. Introduce humor with appropriate frequency.

9

The Task Side of
Team Leadership

In addition to doing an outstanding job of taking care of the human aspects of leadership, breakthrough team leaders concentrate on the task to be performed. They guide the team toward getting its mission and goals accomplished, while at the same time keeping team members motivated and happy. Breakthrough team leaders do not think of being people-oriented versus task-oriented. Instead, they help create a situation in which committed, strongly motivated people pull together to achieve high performance. The needs of people and the demands of the task are juggled simultaneously to achieve good results.

In the previous chapter, I highlighted key aspects of dealing with the human side of team leadership. Here the focus shifts to how the team leader deals with the major aspects of guiding the group in performing its key tasks. You will be spared, however, from a lengthy description of goal setting because such information is well known and well accepted. As a starting point in thinking about the task aspects of team leadership, take the accompanying self-quiz.

The Leadership Task Scale

Directions: Respond to the following statements as they relate to your leadership experience. If you do not have leadership experience, on or off the job, imagine how you would act if you were a team leader. Indicate the extent to which you perform the actions described in the following statements: very infrequently (VI); infrequently (I); sometimes (S); frequently (F); very frequently (VF). Circle the number under the most accurate answer for each question.

	VI	I	S	F	VF
1. I state explicitly what the team is attempting to accomplish.	1	2	3	4	5
2. I work closely with team members in translating the mission into goals.	1	2	3	4	5
3. I'm a "hands off" leader who lets team members figure out how to do things on their own.	5	4	3	2	1
4. I carefully schedule work activities.	1	2	3	4	5
5. I involve myself with the people aspects of the group and let alone the technical details of team activities.	5	4	3	2	1
6. I help others to plan their work down to the intimate details.	1	2	3	4	5
7. Before I leave work, I check to see how much the team has accomplished for the day.	1	2	3	4	5
8. I worry a lot about the details of what the team is working on.	1	2	3	4	5
9. I use a computerized file to check on the status of team projects.	1	2	3	4	5
10. I use Gantt (time and activity) charts to follow the progress of team activities.	1	2	3	4	5
11. I try out new ideas for work improvement.	1	2	3	4	5
12. I point out quality errors when I find them.	1	2	3	4	5
13. I assign tasks to team members.	1	2	3	4	5
14. My team members assign tasks to themselves without my assistance.	5	4	3	2	1
15. Team members decide on their own deadlines.	5	4	3	2	1

	VI	I	S	F	VF
16. I maintain a file of updated job descriptions.	1	2	3	4	5
17. I encourage team members to decide for themselves what is a fair day's work.	1	2	3	4	5
18. I encourage team members to figure out the best method for accomplishing work.	5	4	3	2	1
19. I set quantity standards for work.	1	2	3	4	5
20. I set quality standards for work.	1	2	3	4	5

Total Score _____

Scoring and interpretation: Add the numbers you have circled, and use the following guide to evaluate the extent to which you emphasize the tasks aspects of team leadership.

85–100   You place considerable emphasis on the team achieving its intended tasks. You could be entering the danger zone in which you place so much emphasis on task accomplishment that your style is incompatible with empowerment and team leadership. Try chilling out and backing off a little, and see what happens. Team productivity might increase.

65–84   You place reasonable emphasis on the task side of team leadership. You are concerned about team productivity, but you give team members enough breathing room so they feel they are part of an empowered team. The balance you achieve may be just right for breakthrough team leadership.

20–64   You may be neglecting the task side of leadership in an attempt to boost team spirit and show that you are a modern, empowering, and people-oriented leader. Watch out that your boss may think you are too laid back and uninvolved. You may need to become more involved in goal setting, planning, scheduling, and controlling.

Establish Demanding Tasks

A major driving force in team success is for the leader to establish demanding tasks for the team to perform. A workable alternative is for the leader to facilitate the group establishing demanding tasks for themselves. Either way, the result is the same. The breakthrough team leader recognizes that high performance stems from the team facing a realistically high challenge. Based upon their studies of more than fifty different teams in thirty companies, Katzenbach and Smith concluded that high performing teams all faced urgent and worthwhile purposes.[1]

The sense of urgency is a form of challenge, which in turn is equivalent to the right amount of stress. You may have observed that good athletic teams perform at their best when facing a formidable—but not overwhelming—opponent. The adrenaline flows, the team is pumped up, but members do not feel so overmatched that they experience negative stress. Work teams are similarly pumped up when they face stiff competition in the form of an urgent and challenging task. Among the challenging tasks or goals facing teams have been the following:

- A goal was set at a Japanese auto manufacturer to reduce defects in the computerized panel signals on automobiles to one in one thousand vehicles. (At the time the demanding task was set, the warranty complaints were running at the rate of fifty per one thousand vehicles.)
- Product development teams at Chrysler Corporation were asked to develop a new generation of automobiles that would capture a sizable share of the market for upscale sedans.
- Production groups at Compaq Computer were asked to reduce costs without sacrificing quality on a new line of personal computers.
- A faculty team at Cornell University was charged with the responsibility of designing a new shortened MBA pro-

1. Jon R. Katzenbach and Douglas K. Smith, "The Discipline of Teams," *Harvard Business Review* (March-April 1993), p. 118.

gram that would attract more students while at the same time meeting the demands of a wide range of employers.

The breakthrough team leader urges the team to raise its sights and discard old notions of what constitutes good performance. The leader of a marketing development team at a savings and loan association told her group, "Thirty days may have been a standard time for processing mortgage applications in the past. Today thirty days is about twenty days too long to remain competitive. I won't accept your looking at problems through the same old lenses. I know we can do better."

Part of establishing a demanding task is to impose a deadline, or have the group impose its own. A team without a deadline can drift into interminable discussions and philosophical debates. During one meeting of a cost-reduction team, one of the members sat back in his chair, looked at the ceiling, and said: "Before we go any further, I don't think we have yet answered the question of whether we *should* be cutting costs." The team member in question may have been right, but top management had already made the decision to cut costs. His questioning of the team's purpose was therefore too late.

Let the Team Know Its Boundaries

Teams are achieving wonderful results, from developing high-performing Saturn automobiles to producing Frito-Lay potato chips. To obtain these good results, team members have the power to engage in activities that were previously the province of management, such as negotiating with vendors and disciplining team members. Despite the good results achieved by teams, the leader must impose limits on their activities. The Saturn team members are not empowered to manufacture a limousine, and the Frito-Lay chip makers are not empowered to jettison chips and shift to pretzels. Nor can team members decide to double their pay or halve their working hours.

The team leader's task activity is to carefully delineate the group's boundaries and limits. Without these limits imposed by the leader, teams can be disruptive to the organization as they make incessant demands that create imbalances in the system. The team leader, after conferring with the next level of management, might establish empowerment boundaries relating to such matters as spending money, how many people can be added to the group, and modification of a product or service.

Management consultant Peter Block sees a danger of empowerment leading to a feeling of entitlement. Team members sometimes interpret empowerment to mean that they can do anything they want. In the name of empowerment, he has heard people ask for the following:

* More pay
* Larger budgets
* More people, more subordinates
* Freedom to pursue strictly personal projects
* Greater recognition and privilege
* Immunity from disappointment of those above
* A risk-free environment[2]

An effective tactic is to discuss the limits to empowerment early in the history of the group and revisit the topic periodically. A graphic illustrating areas of empowerment and nonempowerment can be useful. A major reason that the leader has to discuss the boundaries to empowerment is that the term *empowerment* is often used as a weapon. If a team member does not like a management decision or practice, the person will contend that it is not within the spirit of empowerment.

Top management at one company initiated a program of paring down the number of suppliers. A project manager complained that this policy violated the empowerment philosophy. She believed that only those people who worked directly with suppliers should have the authority over the number of suppliers the company could use.

2. List from Peter Block, *Stewardship: Choosing Service Over Self-Interest* (San Francisco: Berrett-Koehler, 1993), p. 34.

Clarify Access to Resources

Another major task responsibility for the team leader is part of setting limits to empowerment. Encouraging people to enthusiastically pursue an idea and informing them later that the project is too expensive is a morale cruncher.[3] Inform the team at the outset of the size of the budget they are working with. You might inform the team, for example, "Our goal is to reduce cycle time by 40 percent with an investment in machinery and consulting fees to a maximum of $350,000."

Access to nonfinancial resources must also be clarified. In a team-based and downsized organization, many new ventures are undertaken without hiring new staff. The team starting up a new activity must therefore use existing company personnel on a part-time or temporary basis. Staff support in the form of clerical workers is also often in short supply. To avoid disappointment and missed deadlines, the team should know in advance the limits to the personnel they will have available to support the project.

Challenge the Team With Fresh Facts and Information

A leader can enhance teamwork by feeding the team valid facts and information that motivate team members to work together to modify the status quo. New information prompts the team to redefine and enrich its understanding of the challenge it is facing. As a result, the team is likely to focus on a common purpose, set clearer goals, and work together more smoothly. Challenging the team with fresh facts and information is therefore another way the breakthrough team leader can deal with the task aspects of leadership.

Feeding relevant facts and information to the team is also valuable because it helps combat groupthink. The team might be prompted by new facts to reexamine a decision it is about

3. "Building an Effective Team," *Working Smart* (February 1994), centerfold page.

to make. A cost-cutting team was about to recommend to top management that every employee in the company take a voluntary 5 percent pay cut. The team leader came upon a management research report indicating that a voluntary pay cut typically led to a plunge in morale and the rapid exit of valuable personnel. After mulling over the results of this research, the groupthink decision on voluntary pay cuts was reversed.

Another example of challenging the team with fresh facts took place at a manufacturing plant. A quality-improvement team recognized the high cost of poor quality. Nevertheless, they did not know what to do next until they researched the different types of defects and established the price of each one. In contrast, teams err when they assume that all the information they need exists within the group.[4]

Assign Task Roles to Team Members

In Chapter 4 I described many different roles played by team members and recommended that you choose among them as the situation dictates. Roles for team players can also be approached from a top-down direction. As a team leader you can assign roles related to task accomplishment. The team members assigned these roles may not have exclusive responsibility for them, yet they should be mindful that their particular talents suit them for fulfilling certain roles.

This section is about task roles, but the presence of various roles also helps develop a spirit of teamwork. Instead of competing against each other, each member contributes in a different way as defined by the role. Roles are not necessarily fixed, and the same team member will occasionally occupy more than one role simultaneously. Virginia Gemmell, director of new products at a creativity consulting firm, observed the following tasks roles in an effective team:

1. An *ideator* is good at generating lots of ideas.
2. An *inventor* takes ideas and translates them into tangible realities, thus being the implementor on the team.

4. Katzenbach and Smith, "The Discipline of Teams," p. 119.

3. A *champion* is someone who has a passion and an impatience for seeing his or her vision become a reality. As a breakthrough team leader, you might assign this role to yourself.
4. A *sponsor* has the power to protect, shield, and encourage both the project and the champion. A sponsor is usually a person of high organizational rank who is not inevitably a member of the team. You will probably need to recruit a company executive to be your sponsor. Your political skills will be needed to attract and retain a sponsor.
5. A technical gatekeeper is a team member who assimilates, accumulates, organizes, and disseminates technical information. This role overlaps considerably with the knowledge contributor role described in Chapter 4.
6. A *market gatekeeper* assimilates, accumulates, organizes, and disseminates market information.

At the start of a project, team members should be encouraged to play multiple task roles, because so much learning needs to take place. By occupying more than one role, the team can magnify its capacity to learn. As the project matures, roles tend to become more defined with team members gravitating toward their roles of greatest expertise.[5]

Use Input From Peer Evaluations

Another task-related activity for leading the team is to encourage high performance by making use of peer evaluations. Depending upon your authority as a team leader, you will have the primary responsibility for evaluating the contribution of each team member. If team members know they will also have responsibility for evaluating each other, they may tend to work even harder. The reason is that team members are often in a better position than the leader to evaluate individual performance within the group.

5. Virginia Gemmell, "Designing a Winning Project Team," *Supervisory Management* (April 1989), pp. 27–28.

Customer service technicians at Xerox Corp. are organized into teams. An elaborate system of peer evaluations plays a key role in performance evaluation. Team members indicate whether a particular aspect of job performance or behavior is a strength or a *developmental opportunity.* A developmental opportunity is a positive way of stating that a person has a weakness. The four factors rated by peers are shown in Exhibit 1. The initials under "Peer Evaluations" refer to the coworkers doing the evaluations. The person being rated thus knows whom to thank (or kick) for the feedback.

Exhibit 1. Peer evaluation of customer service technician.

PERSON EVALUATED: Leslie Fantasia

Skill Categories and Expected Behaviors	Peer Evaluations for Each Category and Behavior					
	TR	JP	CK	JT	CJ	ML
Customer Care						
Takes ownership for customer problems	O	S	S	S	S	S
Follows through on customer commitments	S	S	S	S	S	S
Technical Knowledge & Skill						
Engages in continuous learning to update technical skills	O	S	S	S	S	O
Corrects problems on the first visit	O	O	S	S	S	S
Team Support						
Actively participates in team meetings	S	S	S	S	O	S
Backs up other team members by taking calls in other areas	S	O	O	S	S	S
Minimal absence	S	O	S	S	O	S

Skill Categories and Expected Behaviors	Peer Evaluations for Each Category and Behavior					
	TR	JP	CK	JT	CJ	ML
Finance Management						
Adheres to team's parts expense process	S	S	S	O	S	S
Passes truck audits	S	S	S	O	S	S

Note: S refers to a strength, O refers to a developmental opportunity.

In addition to indicating whether a job factor is a strength or an opportunity, raters can supply comments and developmental suggestions. For example, CJ made the following written comment about Leslie Fantasia: "Missed 50 percent of our team meetings. Should attend team member training and review our team meeting ground rules."

Although peer evaluations fit the spirit of empowerment, they also have some disadvantages. Team members may engage heavily in political behavior to get each other to evaluate them highly. As part of the exchange and bargaining tactic, they may reach informal agreements to evaluate each other highly. If the peer evaluation systems results in the proverbial mutual admiration society, be ready to discount the input. Furthermore, you may want to confront the problem and threaten to disband peer evaluations.

Minimize Micromanagement

A final aspect of task leadership for the breakthrough team leader is to avoid closely monitoring minor details of team member activities. To achieve breakthrough status, the leader must give team members the opportunity to manage their own work. Avoiding micromanagement is a core ingredient to employee empowerment because empowered workers are given considerable latitude to manage their own activities. What specifically constitutes micromanagement depends on team members' perception of the leader's actions. As a tentative guideline, you know you are micromanaging when you regularly do such things as:

- Ask to review the To Do lists of team members.
- Require that team members sign in and sign out for lunch.
- Review all petty cash expenses.
- Require daily progress reports from each team member.
- Ask for the raw data behind reports so you can recalculate the figures used to arrive at conclusions.
- Edit and proofread all reports sent outside the team.
- Visit each member of the team at his or her work area at least once per day.
- Almost always accompany a team member when he or she visits a client or customer for the first time.
- Conduct three-hour performance appraisals.
- Conduct meetings more than twice per week.
- Dictate what software team members should use to prepare reports.
- Investigate in person a site chosen for a team party before giving approval.
- Make food and exercise recommendations to team members.

Minimizing micromanagement helps maximize the contribution of team members. Teams are organized with autonomy for team members in mind. If the leader micromanages the group, team members might be disgruntled. As a result they might not be as productive and creative as they would if given more latitude. Being a micromanager also carries a political disadvantage. In the changing workplace, it is distinctly insulting to be labeled a micromanager. (In the more traditional workplace to be labeled a micromanager is an asset—it implies you maintain tight control over operations and personnel.)

Before moving on to a summary game plan for becoming a breakthrough team player, use the following list to review key ideas about task leadership for the team.

The Task Side of Team Leadership

1. Establish demanding tasks.
2. Let the team know its boundaries.
3. Clarify access to resources.
4. Challenge the team with fresh facts and information.
5. Assign task roles to team members.
6. Use input from peer evaluations.
7. Minimize micromanagement.

10

A Game Plan for Breaking Through

An effective game plan will help you gain maximum advantage from the information presented about becoming a breakthrough team player and team leader. Using the many suggestions in this book, one by one as needed, should help you achieve breakthrough status. But keeping a workable game plan or strategy in mind will enhance your chances for success.

Understanding the game plan will require only a few minutes of your time, but its implementation will be a career-long process if you remain in team-based organizations. The game plan, or model, is shown in Exhibit 2, and follows these general steps: Starting at the left, your many different contributions as a team player (and sometimes a team leader) make it possible for your team to achieve high performance. One more step, however, is required for you to convert membership on a high-performing team into breakthrough status for yourself. You also need to establish links with key people in your organization and the external environment. Details about the model are presented next.

Your contributions and inputs to your team as a player or leader go beyond simply working hard, you also have to work smart. Working smart in this context means understanding the type of contributions that are important to helping the team achieve high performance. The type of attitudes and behaviors that contribute to success as an individual contributor are similar but not identical to those required for team success. Key contributions and inputs to team success include the following (all of which have been described previously in this book):

Exhibit 2. The game plan for becoming a breakthrough team player.

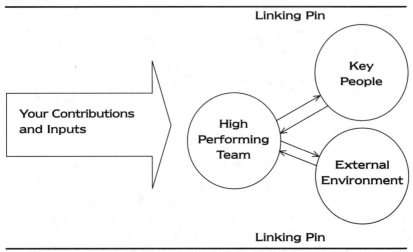

- Technical expertise
- High-quality decisions
- Original ideas, including building on the ideas of others
- Assuming responsibility for problems
- Commitment to team goals
- Seeing the big picture
- Lending a hand during peak workloads
- High level of cooperation and collaboration
- Grabbing the leadership reins (emerging as the informal leader)
- Giving the group useful and valid information
- Serving as an internal process consultant
- Using a cross-functional perspective in solving problems
- Resolving conflicts within the team
- Putting team goals ahead of personal inconvenience
- Encouraging the use of systematic problem-solving within the group
- Helping shape the team's vision and mission
- Introducing humor appropriately
- Establishing demanding tasks for the group

The contributions and inputs just listed help the work group achieve the status of a high-performing team. Such a team achieves high productivity, quality, and morale. Productivity and quality are obviously necessary outputs for a high-performing team. Morale is important, because unless team members achieve reasonable satisfaction they may ultimately burn out and team performance will be lowered.

Contributing to high performance sets the stage for you to become the breakthrough team player or leader. The back-and-forth arrows in Exhibit 2 to/from the key people carry an important message. Assume that your goal is to be identified as a major contributor to the success of the team. A sensible way to accomplish this is to inform key people, such as senior executives and major stockholders, of how well your team is performing. If you hold the formal title of team leader, this liaison role (a linking pin between key people and the team) is readily understandable. A senior executive would ordinarily think that the team leader is the natural spokesperson for the group.

As a team member, you can also be a linking pin. Inform your teammates and team leader of what you are doing. For example, you might explain that you have a good working relationship with a particular executive and that you would like to keep that person informed of the team's activities. Given that you have already established trust with teammates, they will not suspect you of a devious activity, such as being a corporate spy reporting on trouble spots.

Observe that in Exhibit 2 an arrow returns back to the team as well as points toward key people. A breakthrough team player brings back nonprivileged information to the team. To bring back information to the team enhances your credibility. You might report back to the team a tidbit such as, "I was telling Jim Waters [the company executive vice president] about our progress in reducing the cycle time in developing peripheral equipment for our major products. He thinks we're working on one of the key developments in the company. He would like to visit us to discuss our progress."

You can enhance your status as an excellent team player or team leader by volunteering to share the successful methods of your teams with other teams. In a team-based organizational culture, information sharing is highly valued. At Bausch & Lomb Inc., for example, about 20 to 50 percent of employees work on problem-solving teams at any one time. Teams are charged with such responsibilities as reducing costs, improving quality, developing new products and services, and even helping the company enter new countries. Before a new team is implemented, one or more prospective team members visit with an existing successful team. The person associated with the success of a team in management's eyes is often consulted first when a new team is formed.

Also, be willing to draw up recommendations for making other teams effective. Spreading around useful information about your team's success will assist you in becoming the person associated with the success of your team.[1]

The other linking pin role depicted in Exhibit 2 completes the game plan. A sophisticated team player stays focused on the external environment to understand how his or her team will be influenced by or will influence the outside world. A project team leader, for example, at Bausch & Lomb uncovered the fact that an estimated 200 million Chinese people need vision correction. Relating this information to company capability, the leader estimates that up to 50 million Chinese are potential buyers of contact lenses (a major B&L product). The project team expects to influence the environment by establishing a strong presence in China. A China joint venture manager has already been appointed to this position.[2]

Getting back to you and your quest to perform exceptionally well as a team player. You will have achieved the status of a breakthrough team player if you can create two important links: one between the outputs of your team and key people, and the other between the outputs and the external environment. With this level of accomplishment behind you, an upcoming assignment might be membership on the top-management team.

1. "Standing Out on a Team," *Executive Strategies* (October 1994), pp. 3–4.
2. Phil Ebersole, "Bausch Showcases Quality Teams," Rochester *Democrat & Chronicle* (October 15, 1994), pp. 4B, 8B.

Bibliography

Block, Peter, *Stewardship: Choosing Service Over Self-Interest* (San Francisco: Berrett-Koehler, 1993), p. 34.

"Building an Effective Team," *Working Smart* (February 1994), center-fold page.

Byrne, John A., "The Horizontal Corporation: It's About Managing Across, Not Up and Down," *Business Week* (December 20, 1993), p. 79.

Conger, Jay A., *The Charismatic Leader: Beyond the Mystiques of Exceptional Leadership* (San Francisco: Jossey-Bass, 1989).

"Creating an Atmosphere of Trust," *Supervisory Management* (September 1994), p. 9.

Denton, D. Keith, "Multi-Skilled Teams Replace Old Work Systems," *HRMagazine* (September 1992), p. 49.

"Don't Let Discord Ruin Your Meetings," *Personal Report for the Executive* (December 15, 1989), p. 3.

Gemmell, Virginia, "Designing a Winning Project Team," *Supervisory Management* (April 1989), pp. 27–28.

Greengard, Samuel, "Reengineering: Out of the Rubble," *Personnel Journal* (December 1993), pp. 48H–48K.

Herman, Stanley M., *A Force of Ones: Reclaiming Individual Power in a Time of Teams, Work Groups, and Other Crowds* (San Francisco: Jossey-Bass Publishers, 1994).

Katzenbach, Jon R., and Douglas K. Smith, "The Discipline of Teams," *Harvard Business Review* (March-April 1993), p. 118.

———, *The Wisdom Teams: Creating the High-Performance Organization* (New York: Harper Business, 1993), p. 193.

"Let Go of Your Ego," *Executive Strategies* (November 1993), p. 7.

Marren, Michael, "Master Your Meetings," *Success* (June 1991), p. 48.

Parker, Glenn M., *Cross-Functional Teams: Working With Allies, Enemies & Other Strangers* (San Francisco: Jossey-Bass Publishers, 1994).

————, Team Players and Teamwork: The New Competitive Business Strategy (San Francisco: Jossey-Bass, 1990).

Quick, Thomas L. Successful Team Building (New York: AMACOM, 1992), pp. 40–52.

Raskas, Daphna R., and Donald C. Hambrick, "Multifunctional Managerial Development: A Framework for Evaluating the Options," Organizational Dynamics (Autumn 1992), p. 8.

Rodgers, T. J., "Scouting for Talent: A Surefire Plan to Capture and Keep Top Performers," Success (December 1993), p. 80.

Schwartz, Andrew E., and Joy Levin, "Better Group Decision Making," Supervisory Magazine (June 1990), p. 4.

"Standing Out on a Team," Executive Strategies (October 1994), pp. 3–4.

"Talking With Dr. Charles Garfield About Empowering Your Team," Working Smart (June 1992), p. 7.

Tomasko, Robert M., Rethinking the Corporation: The Architecture of Change (New York: AMACOM, 1993), pp. 160–161.

Vroom, Victor H., and Arthur G. Jago, The New Leadership: Managing Participation in Organizations (Englewood Cliffs, N.J.: Prentice-Hall, 1988).

Walsh, Richard J., "Ten Basic Counseling Skills," Supervisory Management (July 1977), p. 9.

Yukl, Gary, Skills for Managers and Leaders: Text, Cases, and Exercises (Englewood Cliffs, N.J.: Prentice-Hall, 1990), pp. 62–63.

Index